VETERANS IN TECH: INNOVATIVE CAREERS FOR ALL GENERATIONS OF VETERANS

HEARING

BEFORE THE

SUBCOMMITTEE ON ECONOMIC OPPORTUNITY

OF THE

COMMITTEE ON VETERANS' AFFAIRS
U.S. HOUSE OF REPRESENTATIVES

ONE HUNDRED FOURTEENTH CONGRESS

SECOND SESSION

TUESDAY, MAY 17, 2016

Serial No. 114–69

Printed for the use of the Committee on Veterans' Affairs

Available via the World Wide Web: http://www.fdsys.gov

U.S. GOVERNMENT PUBLISHING OFFICE

25–180   WASHINGTON : 2017

For sale by the Superintendent of Documents, U.S. Government Publishing Office
Internet: bookstore.gpo.gov   Phone: toll free (866) 512–1800; DC area (202) 512–1800
Fax: (202) 512–2104   Mail: Stop IDCC, Washington, DC 20402–0001

Pursuant to clause 2(e)(4) of rule XI of the Rules of the House, public hearing records of the Committee on Veterans' Affairs are also published in electronic form. **The printed hearing record remains the official version.** Because electronic submissions are used to prepare both printed and electronic versions of the hearing record, the process of converting between various electronic formats may introduce unintentional errors or omissions. Such occurrences are inherent in the current publication process and should diminish as the process is further refined.

CONTENTS

Tuesday, May 17, 2016

VETERANS IN TECH: INNOVATIVE CAREERS FOR ALL GENERATIONS OF VETERANS

Tuesday, May 17, 2016

COMMITTEE ON VETERANS' AFFAIRS,
U. S. HOUSE OF REPRESENTATIVES,
Washington, D.C.

The Subcommittee met, pursuant to notice, at 3:02 p.m., in Room 334, Cannon House Office Building, Hon. Brad Wenstrup [Chairman of the Subcommittee] presiding.

Present: Representatives Wenstrup, Takano, Zeldin, Costello, Radewagen, Bost, and McNerney.

OPENING STATEMENT OF BRAD WENSTRUP, CHAIRMAN

Mr. WENSTRUP. Good afternoon, everyone. The Subcommittee will come to order. I want to thank you all for waiting for us, for one, but I thank you all for joining us here today for our hearing entitled "Veterans in Tech: Innovative Careers For All Generations of Veterans."

As more servicemembers continue to transition out of the military and into civilian life, it is important that we assist them into meaningful careers and not just into jobs. And while the unemployment rates among veterans continue to decline or remain stagnant, it is vital that we inform our transitioning servicemembers and veterans of all ages of the career opportunities within all sectors of the economy, especially the ever-growing and unique opportunities within the tech sector.

As startups and innovative businesses continue to inundate the economy more and more each day, we need to ensure that veterans are made aware of the job opportunities within this sector, as well as the sector's need and desire for veteran employees. We are highlighting the tech industry today because I know that the flexibility these jobs offer, as well as the skills needed to be successful in these careers, make veterans an obvious fit for these positions and trades.

Furthermore, as Amazon highlighted in their written testimony, this field of work is also an optimal opportunity for military spouses to find a career that is flexible and portable for the lifestyle of a military spouse. These careers offer great opportunities that are much better than the temporary jobs that many military spouses are forced to take, due to the mobility associated with military service.

It is obvious that companies like the groups before us here today, recognize the benefits of training and employing more veterans and the skills that they bring to the table. I believe, however, that more

(1)

needs to be done at the outset, as these men and women are first exiting the military to make them aware of what the tech space has to offer and their professional potential in these unique careers.

We need to figure out how to connect these individuals to companies as well as get them into the necessary training programs to cover any skill gaps that may exist before entering the tech field. There is obviously a great potential in a working partnership between our Nation's veterans and tech companies, but we need to better work together to make this connection happen as early as possible.

While it is important that we continue to connect transitioning servicemembers to these lucrative tech careers, we would be remiss if we didn't also address ways to connect older veterans to the opportunities that the tech industry has to offer. These veterans bring forth similar experiences and skills as many of our younger veterans do, and I hope that we can all work together and brainstorm ways to train and place veterans of all eras and of all ages into tech jobs.

It is also important that as we discuss how to better recruit and retain veterans in this field, that we also ensure that we are not only placing a veteran in a job, but we are training them and honing their skills so they are promotable, and can truly have a successful career in this ever-growing sector. So I look forward to our discussion this afternoon. I believe I speak for every Member of this Subcommittee when I say that we appreciate everything our four panelists here today are doing for the men and women who have served, and your work to train, employ, and promote veterans within your companies.

I will now yield to my colleague, Ranking Member Takano, for any opening statement he may have.

OPENING STATEMENT OF MARK TAKANO, RANKING MEMBER

Mr. TAKANO. Thank you, Mr. Chairman, for holding this hearing today on how veterans can access careers in the high-growth tech sector of our economy.

We know that many veterans are excellent prospects for these highly desirable jobs because of the skills and training they received in the military. Because tech jobs tend to be career jobs, we are here today to understand what the tech industry needs and wants in a full-time employee, how tech employees find qualified veteran prospects, what they are doing to support veterans after providing that pathway in, and what role the Federal government should play in making tech sector opportunities available to more veterans, particularly veterans from the Gulf War and Vietnam War eras.

I want to welcome the four witnesses this afternoon. I look forward to their testimony and the opportunity to ask questions, and I really want to thank the Chairman for working with the minority in scheduling this hearing. I think it is going to be a great hearing this afternoon. Thank you.

Mr. WENSTRUP. Thank you, Mr. Takano, and I agree with you.

I now want to recognize our first and only panel of witnesses today. First, with us today we have Mr. Bernard Bergan, a Technical Account Manager for Microsoft; Mr. Brian Huseman, Vice President of Public Policy for Amazon; Vice Admiral Joseph Kernan, Chairman of NS2 Serves; and Mr. Todd Bowers, Director of UberMILITARY.

Mr. Bergan, I want to thank you for your service in uniform, in the United States Army, and let's begin with you. You have five minutes for your opening statement.

STATEMENT OF BERNARD BERGAN

Mr. BERGAN. Thank you, Chairman Wenstrup, Ranking Member Takano, and Members of the Subcommittee. My name is Bernard Bergan, I am an Army veteran, a graduate of the Microsoft Software and Systems Academy, and currently work at Microsoft as a Technical Account Manager.

I am also an example of how tech companies can make a significant impact on veterans by helping them discover meaningful career paths as they reenter civilian life. Veterans face enormous challenges transitioning into the private sector. That is why, two years ago, Microsoft launched the MSSA Program, and I was one of the first graduates. Since then we have announced that the program is expanding into 12 locations around the country, and Microsoft has pledged to train and find careers for 5,000 servicemembers in the IT sector over the next five years.

Like many other veterans, I didn't get here on my own. I have been fortunate to have some great mentors. When I was 12 years old, I moved from the United States Virgin Islands with my parents and brothers to Virginia, where I attended high school and graduated from Old Dominion University with a criminal justice degree. I then decided to pursue an opportunity in the United States Army. I am proud to say I was on active duty from 2008 to 2014, serving all over the world, including an 11-month deployment in Afghanistan's Helmand province.

My experience taught me the importance of teamwork and deeply instilled the value of selfless service and a commitment to excellence. I came home in May of 2013, and it was tough for me and my family because I didn't know where my next job would be. I was then introduced to the MSSA Program by my commanding officer at Joint Base Lewis-McChord, Colonel Charles Hodges. Colonel Hodges displayed leadership and took a chance on me. The intensive IT skills training paired with a guarantee of a job interview with Microsoft made the program my most attractive option.

Working at Microsoft has been incredibly rewarding. Each day allows me to interact with passionate individuals who work to have a global impact as they innovate around solving problems. The teamwork, camaraderie, and expertise I enjoy here at Microsoft is similar to my time in the Army, and makes me feel more at home than I could ever have imagined.

The MSSA has also been good for my family. Once I settled into my new career, my wife was able to focus on hers. She is now headed back to school to pursue her MBA. Looking back, it is fair to say it has not been a particularly easy transition out of the military. I was uncertain about how I would know I was making the right career move. A transition from the military is a family affair. While much of my testimony has focused on veteran employment, it is also important to understand military spouse employment. Spouses make tremendous sacrifices, especially when their loved one is deployed. For its part, Microsoft recognizes that more must be done to help spouses. And to that end, the company will be establishing a community-based model of our MSSA that will offer evening courses, making them more available to working spouses who may want to make a career change.

In conclusion, I am so proud of the work the Microsoft Military Affairs Team is doing to empower veterans like me with education and relevant skills training that leads to high-paying IT careers. It is past time for industry, government, and nonprofit leaders to give back to our veterans. I want to leave you with three observations. First, this program works. I am a testament to that. Second, it works because mentoring has proven to be a critical part of the MSSA program. And third, the MSSA program is attractive to servicemembers because it provides relevant training that leads to meaningful, high-paying IT careers.

Thank you again for the opportunity to testify this afternoon to provide a voice for those transitioning from the military back into civilian life. I look forward to answering your questions.

[THE PREPARED STATEMENT OF BERNARD BERGAN APPEARS IN THE APPENDIX]

Mr. WENSTRUP. Thank you, Mr. Bergan.

Mr. Huseman, you are now recognized for five minutes.

STATEMENT OF BRIAN HUSEMAN

Mr. HUSEMAN. Thank you, Chairman Wenstrup, and Ranking Member Takano, and other Members of the Subcommittee. My name is Brian Huseman, and I am Amazon's Vice President of Public Policy. Thank you for holding this hearing on this important topic.

I would like to highlight three issues. First, Amazon's commitment to hiring veterans. Second, our commitment to training veterans once at the company, including our innovative Career Choice Program. And finally, our recommendations for expanding jobs for veterans in the tech sector.

First, Amazon is strongly committed to hiring veterans. Our mission is to be the world's most customer-centric company. And to accomplish this, we are constantly looking for leaders who can invent and think big, or have bias for action, and deliver results on behalf of our customers. And as you know, these principles look very familiar to the men and women who have served in the armed forces.

Amazon actively recruits U.S. military veterans to fill roles across the company, from our corporate offices to our fulfillment network. Since 2011, we have hired over 10,000 veterans. And earlier this month, as part of the fifth anniversary of the Joining Forces Initiative, we announced that we will hire 25,000 additional veterans and military spouses over the next five years, the largest pledge of any technology company. We also recently pledged to train 10,000 servicemembers, veterans, and military spouses in cloud computing, which offers a path to Amazon Web Services Certification, an industry-recognized certification program in this high-demand field. This training includes hands-on experiences with the

Amazon Web Services platform, including free access to labs and a wide library of content for learning about the cloud.

We believe this commitment is the smart thing to do for our veterans and military spouses, for Amazon, and for our hundreds of millions of customers. As a son and grandson of veterans, I am excited to be a small part of hiring and training these incredible leaders.

Second, our commitment to the military does not end once candidates are hired. Once employed at Amazon, we connect them with our internal employee network of veterans that we call the Amazon Warriors, which allows them to share experiences and receive mentoring and gain exposure to career and development opportunities.

I also want to highlight our innovative Career Choice Program, which is something we are very proud of. Veterans and military spouses in eligible Amazon roles can enroll in the Career Choice Program, where we will prepay 95 percent of tuition and fees for courses related to in-demand fields, and that is regardless of whether the skills are relevant to a career at Amazon. So we exclusively fund education in high-demand fields as determined by the U.S. Bureau of Labor Statistics. And so far, thousands of employees have participated in the Career Choice Program, and our first Career Choice graduate is now a nurse in Kentucky.

Finally, we have two principal recommendations we would like to offer. First, we recommend that active duty servicemembers have the opportunity to take advantage of private sector technical training program in fields like cloud computing before they depart from service, as they may not have had experience with the latest software and systems used by the private sector. Also, many separating servicemembers are excellent candidates for careers in high tech, even though their backgrounds might not be technical. Without technical training before separation, they may never explore careers in the tech sector.

Second, we recommend expansion of partnerships between the military and the private sector. One such program, Camo2Commerce, has been very successful in providing career development and jobs to servicemembers transitioning out of the Joint Base Lewis-McChord, which is in Amazon's home state of Washington. Our Amazon Web services recruiters regularly seek out graduates of this training program, and we believe it should serve as a model for other military installations and communities.

In conclusion, we are committed to hiring veterans, and have pledged to hire an additional 25,000 over the next five years. We also have a strong commitment to training our veteran employees, and we are excited that some of them might participate in our innovative Career Choice education program. And we believe that more can be done to provide technical training before service separation and to increase partnerships with the private sector. Our veteran and military spouse employees are a tremendous asset for our company and our customers, and we are very excited to see what the next 25,000 will create over the next few years.

So thank you for calling this hearing and inviting us to testify.

[THE PREPARED STATEMENT OF BRIAN HUSEMAN APPEARS IN THE APPENDIX]

Mr. WENSTRUP. Well, thank you, Mr. Huseman.

And Admiral Kernan, thank you for your many years of service in the Navy. And you are now recognized for five minutes.

STATEMENT OF VICE ADMIRAL JOSEPH KERNAN

Vice Admiral KERNAN. Chairman Wenstrup, Ranking Member Takano, and Members of the Subcommittee, my name is Joseph Kernan, I am a retired Navy Vice Admiral. I am currently the Senior Vice President of Corporate Development and Marketing at SAP National Security Services. It is an honor to be with you here today to testify in my other role as Chairman of NS2 Serves, a nonprofit training and employment program for veterans. My commitment to this issue stems from my 36 plus years of service in naval, special operations, joint, and interagency organizations in combat, during disaster relief, or in peaceful conditions, but always serving alongside those that we are discussing today.

I think we would all agree today veterans who choose to devote a portion of their lives to protecting and serving our Nation deserve opportunities to thrive in the civilian sector. They have a wide variety of work-life skills, but transitioning to the civilian workforce is often daunting, particularly for young, enlisted servicemembers. They do not want a handout, but rather an opportunity for a fresh start in their post-military lives for themselves and for their families. The information technology field is one of many ideally suited to veterans, regardless of their occupational specialty while they were serving in the military.

In the Department of Defense, commercial technology is used to manage mission planning, human resources, weapons systems, operations and maintenance, supply chains, and finance. Most of these functions are common to virtually every commercial business. However, veterans' character traits, developed at a very young age while they are serving, are the extraordinary differentiator for new hire considerations in the commercial sector. They strive to be leaders. They learn how to work as a team, and they understand how foundational that is to achieving success in virtually any endeavor. They constantly learned and mastered a multitude of cross-functional skills and quickly adapted in dynamic environments. Possibly, most notably, is their grasp and acceptance of accountability, accountability for their decisions and accountability to their organizations, their leadership, and their fellow workers.

About the NS2 service program that I chair. SAP National Security Services funded and established this nonprofit organization in 2014, specifically to train and find employment for veterans in high-tech careers. We as well actively seek non-government, commercial partners to scale the program. Our program targets enlisted men and women from all military services and all sub-specialties. We arm graduates with SAP technology certifications and with other transition attributes, so that they can compete well for technology support jobs in the thousands of companies and government organizations that utilize SAP products.

The NS2 Serves program has many key differentiators. All of the details of the program I provided in my written testimony. The program is an in-resident, 11-week program. The veterans pay nothing for the program. They just need to arrive with the will to succeed.

It leverages the veterans' penchant for teamwork. Participants can and do help each other with transition and with academics. The CEO and virtually every member of our 400 plus person company is an active mentor in this program. Graduates, with their consultant certifications, have all been hired into government or commercial jobs with a minimum starting salary of $60,000, inclusive of medical and retirement benefits. By the end of this week, we will have graduated 100 graduates from nearly 20 states, some disabled, several with service dogs, at a cost of approximately $15,000 per student. This is a worthwhile investment for substantive career, family, emotional stability, stress relief, self-confidence, and the potential avoidance of dependence on Federal and State support programs.

A few recommendations. A more robust centralized job opportunity Web site like veterans.gov, but easily accessible and usable, managed under the strong proactive partnership between government and commercial industry, with its utility measured by employment statistics across all demographics of veterans. The Defense Department should shepherd veterans into this site before their separation.

Investing in veterans. I would advocate our model program. Every graduate is in a career-centric job at no financial expense to the veteran or to their GI bill benefits. The commercial sector can take this task on similarly.

Job qualifications. For commercial sector H.R. departments, veterans should be better valued for their military education, their experience, and their work ethic. They remain extraordinarily educatable and motivated, they just need the opportunity.

Mr. Chairman, Ranking Member Takano, Members of the Subcommittee, I would again like to thank you for the opportunity to testify today. Veterans have much more to offer this country above that which they have already given. Thank you for your continued public service and for what you do for veterans. I am happy to answer any questions. Thank you.

[THE PREPARED STATEMENT OF VICE ADMIRAL JOSEPH KERNAN APPEARS IN THE APPENDIX]

Mr. WENSTRUP. Well, thank you very much, Admiral.

And lastly, Mr. Bowers, I want to thank you for your service in the United States Marine Corps, and you are now recognized for five minutes.

STATEMENT OF TODD BOWERS

Mr. BOWERS. Thank you, sir. Mr. Chairman, Ranking Member, and Members of the Committee, thank you so much for inviting me here today to talk to you about the UberMILITARY Program and our endeavors to support veterans and military families as they go through the many transitions, many of which I went through myself. It has been many years since I sat before this Committee and it is an honor and privilege to be back. I actually think I am sitting in the exact same chair, so that is exciting as well.

I would like to take a few moments and share with you why I am here today, how I became involved with the UberMILITARY program. It was during my second tour in Iraq when I found myself on the outskirts of Fallujah and was pinned behind a Humvee. That Humvee eventually pulled away and took away my cover as a rifle—my rifle scope was hit by a sniper's bullet. Needless to say, the marine that drove away did not get a five star rating. I really hoped that one would stick a little better.

It was a few months later, though, that I found myself back in Washington, D.C. after these incredible experiences overseas, and I was preparing to go back to school. As a proud community college student, I was taking the next step to be able to finish my degree, and I found a window between the time that I came home to when classes started. I had to work small jobs here and there that didn't have flexible timing, didn't have the right sort of work that I was looking for to be able to make that transition back into school. I really needed something to fill that gap. This time really impacted my life greatly. It was a time when I was already dealing with trying to transition back, and not having that flexibility and mobility with respect to timing for work opportunities impacted me greatly.

Traditionally, veterans during this time end up spending their hard-earned savings. They end up going into credit card debt. They end up basically sitting back and spending all of their hard-earned money to be able to fill this window of time. This is what inevitably led me to the UberMILITARY Program. In September 2014, Uber announced that we were aiming to partner with 50,000 members of the military community to include their families. We created this target because we knew the skills, the work ethic, and integrity exemplified by our Nation's veterans was unmatched. Frankly, we knew this would be good for business. This was based on data tracking that we did in cities with high veteran populations, similar to San Diego, where we knew that compared to their civilian peers, veterans that were driving on the platform had longer supply hours and higher customer ratings.

Focusing on veterans and military families was a business decision, but more importantly, it was a way to empower this community with a flexibility and mobility that they had never had before. After just under 18 months of engaging with the military community, Uber achieved its goal six weeks ahead of schedule. As of this morning, more than 56,000 self-identified veterans and military family members have signed up to drive with Uber, and over 50 percent of them have taken a trip on the platform. All of that work has resulted in an astounding $155 million worth of earnings since we started tracking this data. That is earnings going directly into their pockets, similar to my situation, at times when they may need it most.

So how did we reach this goal? To start, we designated engaged with more than 60 UberMILITARY Program leaders from our city-based teams, many of which are veterans themselves. These individuals led the charge in their respective cities, working with local and national organizations, base commanders, and community leaders. We partnered with Blue Chip organizations that support the military community, such as the Chamber of Commerce Hiring our Heroes Program, the Blue Star Families and the American Military Families Association, to name a few. We also created the UberMILITARY Advisory Board, which was chaired by former Secretary of Defense Bob Gates, with the likes of General Stanley

McChrystal, Admiral Eric Olson, and many others that have helped guide us through this program.

As we look to the future of UberMILITARY, we are setting new goals, thanks to all of the work that we have done thus far that will impact this community. Our new mission is as follows: 500 million in earnings to drive our partners who have served in the military and their families by 2020; next, increased access to reliable transportation in and around military communities to reduce alcohol-related incidents on and around these communities; finally, make Uber even more rewarding for the drivers with military backgrounds.

I would like to conclude my testimony today on a little bit more of a personal note as well. After leaving service, I knew that I wanted to do something that would truly make a difference in the lives of veterans and their families. I knew that by fulfilling this dream, and being able to continue to engage with those that I served with, there would be unique opportunities that would come up. That unique opportunity is the Uber platform. It is something that we have never seen before that can support this community in a very different manner, and I believe it is having a profound impact on veterans and military families. I am proud to say that a technology platform of this nature has never economically empowered this community in such a manner before, and I am excited that this is just the beginning.

As we continue our mission, I am enthusiastic to go to work every day, and provide the opportunities that our veterans and military families deserve. I would like to thank you all for your time. I look forward to any questions, and please refer to my testimony for additional details. Thank you.

[THE PREPARED STATEMENT OF TODD BOWERS APPEARS IN THE APPENDIX]

Mr. WENSTRUP. I thank you all for your remarks, and I am going to now yield myself five minutes for questions. I do appreciate some of the things I heard here today, talking about recognizing capabilities and possibilities for our veterans beyond their military specialty. And I think that is important to recognize, because they bring a lot of talents to the plate and can be trained into virtually any field if given the opportunity.

Mr. Bowers, just a quick question for you. Will we be seeing a icon on our choices for vehicle and driver to say Uber veteran or UberMILITARY at some time in the future?

Mr. BOWERS. So we have actually looked at this endeavor, but what I would like to point to is something that we actually did on Veterans Day where we allowed our veteran partner drivers, riders, everybody who is engaged on the Uber app on Veterans Day to understand the sacrifices that these individuals have made. We worked with the Joining Forces Initiative to raise money to help homeless veterans get to and from employment opportunities. We did this by working very closely with the National Coalition of Homeless Veterans, to identify groups that had transportation issues, and it was a huge success. That was a way that we are able to look at the technology platform and be able to identify what we can do to be able to have an impact on our riders and drivers.

One of the things we have been exploring is the opportunity to allow veterans to, basically, connect with riders and let them know that they are a veteran on the front end of the trip. This is something that we have been thinking about for some time. But what we found that I think is rather unique is—we get very caught up in being the digital tool. But it is when you get in that car that you end up asking the individual that is driving you, "Hey, how come you drive with Uber?" And a tremendous amount of veterans that drive on the platform love that opportunity to engage with their civilian peers, and really start to acclimatize back into civilian life, just by having candid conversations with individuals behind the wheel.

So it is something that we are definitely looking at, it is something that we think would be rather unique, and I would like to go as far as to be able to say what branch of service they are in, because you know, no bias, but being a Marine, it is a pretty proud thing to be in.

Mr. WALSTRUP. Well, I will just answer that with a hooah. But, anyway.

Admiral, NS2 Serves is focusing on enlisted servicemembers. What is the reason for that? Is there a distinct advantage, or are you trying to create more opportunity for enlisted?

Vice Admiral KERNAN. I think the latter. I mean the, you know, the unemployment rate for enlisted men and women across all services is higher than everyone else in the service. So I think we, you know, as a smaller company, we wanted to focus somewhere where we essentially transition from kind of a blue-collar to a white-collar, so. And again, recognizing the qualities that they have and their ability to learn, particularly as a team, we thought we would focus on them and so that is kind of our initial focus.

The others that have access to the course, gold star spouses are as well acceptable into the course and we certainly—we have had, actually, two young junior officers go through the program, so we don't cut them out, but they were extraordinary cases where they had significant, you know, PTS type situations and were looking for something to do, and so they are off and on their way in great careers.

Mr. WENSTRUP. Excellent.

Mr. Bergan, when someone graduates from your academy, what type of positions are they qualified to take on?

Mr. BERGAN. Thank you for the question, Mr. Chairman. What differentiates the Microsoft Software and Systems Academy is our learnings track. When I attended the Microsoft Software and Systems Academy, I took the software development learning track. So after my 16 weeks, I interviewed with Microsoft specifically for a software development job. There is also going to be five different learning tracks where you would have CRM, Power BI, and some of the other high in-demand roles that we are seeing within our company that we will need to fill over the next five years.

Mr. WENSTRUP. Thank you. And it sounds like each of you, and you may want to comment quickly in the little time we have left, are making efforts to not employ veterans, but to retain them and promote them up the chain. And we will start with you, Mr. Huseman.

Mr. HUSEMAN. Yes, we think it is important to provide career mentorship activities once veterans are hired. Our Amazon Warriors Network, internal employee network we think is very valuable to that, to provide coaching once they are on board. Also, our Career Choice Program, which is something that we are very excited about, provides our employees with the opportunity to get an education in an in-demand field, and that is regardless of whether that is relevant to a career at Amazon.

Mr. WENSTRUP. Thank you. If anyone else would care to comment on the structure of your programs, I would appreciate it real quick.

Vice Admiral KERNAN. Yeah, I think creating, you know, just creating the opportunity for them to get in the works—I don't worry about young men and women veterans as far as competing with everyone else. They will do extraordinarily well. They have that penchant as well to like to win and try to overacheive. And so thus far our program has only been in place for two years now, but the feedback from employers is extraordinary. Every single one of them have been very, very positive. They will work their way up and its career opportunities for the rest of their lives.

Mr. WENSTRUP. Mr. Bergan?

Mr. BERGAN. And if I can speak to that really quickly, Mr. Chairman. I have only been with Microsoft for two years and I have been promoted twice since getting there. The continued mentorship and support of the Microsoft military community coupled with just our career training and advancement programs within the company is something I just really took advantage of and tested. And it has proven to be a very valuable opportunity and it is one of our transition stories that we really try to champion to veterans looking for the same opportunities.

Mr. WENSTRUP. I now recognize the Ranking Member for any questions he may have.

Mr. TAKANO. Thank you, Mr. Chairman. Mr. Bowers, thank you for your service and your continued commitment to helping veterans, and to find an easier way than you had going to school and supporting yourself. I want to ask you one question. Do you have any information on Uber use among veterans attempting to get to a VA facility for an appointment?

Mr. BOWERS. This is something that we have been discussing quite a bit to be able to understand how we could help the VA solve some of their transportation issues. So I would love to be able to follow-up with you with some more detail. I don't have it directly in front of me, but we have been looking at veterans who have been using getting to and from VA facilities. We are able to do something that is rather unique where we can actually geo tag around VA facilities and identify where veterans may be getting dropped off.

This is something that we think would be incredibly useful. And we have been in discussions with the VA about how we can possibly pilot a program specifically that would help veterans get to and from their appointments. In MilCon/VA there is actually some language that is put in there that actually gives the VA the authorization to be able to pilot some of these programs with us.

Mr. TAKANO. Well, great. As you know it has been a big issue with our—

Mr. BOWERS. Yes, sir.

Mr. TAKANO [continued]. —health appointments. Mr. Bernard, thank you for your service as well, and especially for your 11-month serving in Helmand Province. What a story that is. You mentioned that some graduates go on to school rather than go straight on to a job after the 16-month training you have with Microsoft. I assume this is where GI Bill benefits come into play; is that true?

Mr. BERGAN. Thank you for that question. For some servicemen and women after they complete their 16 weeks, we do earn credit hours. And for them going on to university is the best option for them and their families. So we have seen that.

Mr. TAKANO. Okay. And to your knowledge are GI Bill benefits being used during MSSA training for any purpose, like obtaining certifications?

Mr. BERGAN. When I went through—I can only speak for my experience. When I went through I used a bit of my GI Bill benefits as a part of the training program. And what I saw that was an investment in me and my family and our future.

Mr. TAKANO. So you were able to use your GI Bill benefits even though you hadn't separated yet from the military?

Mr. BERGAN. That is correct.

Mr. TAKANO. Okay. At some point I would like to understand more about that. I think the Committee should look into that. I am also interested in your comment that the skills you acquired in the Microsoft Software and Systems Academy, the MSSA program, they were not Microsoft specific, but rather industry-recognized credentials that would allow you portability. Can you expand on this issue some and give us an idea of what skills are involved that you learned?

Mr. BERGAN. Thank you again for that question. One thing I really enjoyed about the Academy when I attended was that you had learning tracks. So I was really interested in software development, app development and developing for the cloud. And that is agnostic to any platform. Once you have those skills in the technology sector, you can take them anywhere.

And each instructor was geared to teaching you how to do this not specifically to a platform. One of the benefits of our mentorship base program was, I got to actually work with software engineers at Microsoft who would show me what they do day to day on the job, which helped me really dial into what I needed to accomplish.

Mr. TAKANO. Well, that is wonderful. Why would Microsoft fund an IT school that feeds other company's talent pipelines? Why would they do that?

Mr. BOWERS. You know, that just touches me really personally, because, you know, when I first heard about this program I thought it was too good to be true. And here I am. You know, when I took it home to my wife she didn't believe me either. And ultimately the Microsoft Military Affairs Department, when they sat with me initially, they said, "Bernard, this is our investment in the veteran's community. We know that you guys are sharp. We know that you are hardworking, you are focused, you are willing to do this. And we are willing to take a chance investing in you."

Mr. TAKANO. Well, do graduates actually get jobs with Microsoft's competitors?

Mr. BERGAN. Absolutely.

Mr. TAKANO. Wow.

Mr. BERGAN. Absolutely.

Mr. TAKANO. What do you think is the major reason you succeeded at Microsoft after graduating from the MSSA?

Mr. BERGAN. I would say, as everyone spoke to up here, that ongoing mentorship is very unique. And our Microsoft military veterans, we really just pool around each other and just support each other's transition goals and our career plans.

Mr. TAKANO. Well, you mentioned the high level of support that you got in Microsoft's Academy in soft skills, like creating a resume and being coached on interviewing. You say that TAP isn't as helpful in these areas because commanding officers need their troops to be on duty until their last day. Do you feel this is a widespread problem? Is it getting better or worse in your opinion?

Mr. BERGAN. That's a very good question. And I can only speak to my experience. In those last few months on active duty you are in a whirlwind of things that must be done and that is department mandated, TAP being one of those things. Where TAP was very helpful in some ways, in my experience it didn't provide me a clear path to what I was going to do next. And that's where the MSSA filled that gap with a clear path of what I was going to be doing next.

Mr. TAKANO. With the Chairman's indulgence, may I ask one more questions, sir? I know that there are pilot programs planned to offer courses in the evening so spouses can attend. Are MSSA courses offered to spouses now?

Mr. BERGAN. At the moment those are plans that we are working with Members of Congress and even with the different districts to figure out how best to implement. And we would love to follow-up with more details on that.

Mr. TAKANO. Great, thank you. I yield back, Mr. Chairman. Thank you for allowing me that extra time.

Mr. WENSTRUP. Mr. Costello, you are recognized for five minutes.

Mr. COSTELLO. I can just pick up where Mr. Takano left off. Can you just describe, Mr. Bergan, the role that your CO played and also how important the referral from your CO was in his awareness with the MSSA program?

Mr. BERGAN. Thank you, Congressman, for that question. For every commanding officer, and the Admiral will speak to that, giving up a body is a very difficult decision. So to have Colonel Hodges' buy-in and belief in myself and the other 22 men and women who attended cohort 1 of this program was losing some of his best servicemen and women, but he saw the importance of making sure our exit out of the military was well planned, just as our entry into the military was. So without that colonel's buy-in— and that would be one of my recommendations, just supporting our senior leaders to make those decisions from base to base on how they assist with their servicemen and women transitioning from the military.

Mr. COSTELLO. Right. You also mentioned something else and I am going to start with Mr. Bowers, whom I want to thank again for taking the time to come meet with me in my office last week. And the question will be directed to all four of you. I thought you really hit on something talking about how important it is for the working spouse to feel that whatever program you are in, whatever employer that you are with, that it is in a location and that from a work/life balance, there is also opportunity for what your spouse may be pursuing or where they are working.

Just describe for me in general terms or be as specific as you would like on what the winning formula is for these types of programs and in the companies that you work for, so that when we speak to other companies, you know, our Members, all of us have companies come in, "We want to be helpful to veterans. We have a veterans set aside program for this or we help them in this way or provide opportunity here." Share with me, if you could, the importance that providing that sort of opportunity or accommodating, if you will, the spouse and the role that it plays in how fulfilled you feel with the company that you are at given that variable.

Mr. BOWERS. So I can speak to the uniqueness that Uber brings to the table with respect to the flexibility and mobility for military spouses. And say that it was about a year ago that we launched the UberMILITARY Families Coalition. And this was a partnership with four organizations: the Chamber of Commerce Hiring our Heroes, Blue Star Families, National Military Families Association, and the American Military Partners Association.

This was borne out of what we discovered, that many military spouses were leaning towards driving with Uber as an opportunity, because the average military family moves eight times over a 20-year career. Never before has there been an opportunity for folks to be able to go into a new town and be able to have that flexibility and mobility, which is driving with Uber.

Additionally, military spouses and families as a whole deal with a tremendous amount during deployments as well. So spouses love the flexibility and mobility about being able to drop the kids off at daycare, or whatever the case may be, while their loved one is deployed. This was very surprising to us. So we are going to continue to focus on military families on and around military installations to make sure that they have this opportunity available to them. We are going to continue our partnerships to make sure that we are getting the word out to folks that this is available.

Really it is at a unique time right now, as we are seeing operational tempo and the number of deployments going down, but we are also seeing the surgence that military families want to be employed. They want to be a part of something. They want to be able to do something for their communities. And the Uber platform seems to be something that they are very interested in. So thank you for your question.

Mr. HUSEMAN. And, Congressman, military spouses are very valuable to Amazon. They have to deal with flexibility and constant change, and those skills do prove valuable to a company like Amazon that is fast changing. We have what we call virtual contact centers, which our customer support specialists that can work from home. And those jobs are very well suited to military spouses.

We also make a focus on providing quality jobs for military spouses. I think one great example is Gen Harrison-Doss, who she leads a team of recruiters based in Seattle from her home in Abilene, Texas where she is stationed with her husband. And she has actually been promoted in the company. And so I think the military spouses bring great skills and we are very proud to have them and to continue to hire them.

Vice Admiral KERNAN. Probably one of the big advantages of the program that I am involved is SAP software is just prolific, and I think the numbers are over nearly 75 percent of all the Fortune 4,000 companies have SAP software. We usually take one or two, hire one or two, SAP North America hires a couple, but most of them go to companies all over—that are anywhere. So I mean, the global ecosystem of SAP who use their enterprise resource planning software or supply chain logistic, virtually every company has that. So that just—in my mind that just creates an extraordinary ecosystem of jobs that veterans can go work at wherever they are.

The other thing, and certainly in technical, you know, virtual, working virtually is very common. I personally do it, as my wife rightly deserves, she gets 51 percent of the vote of where I live after our 27 moves. And so I think the technology community and the ability to work virtually, and in our case, candidly, I am somewhat agnostic to where the veterans find jobs. I don't really care. I just want them to get good viable work where they can take care of their families and their families have opportunities.

Our hope is—my hope personally is that our program is—we can expand it and build it that spouses are as well available to the course. At this point, in its kind of youth infant stages, you know, we are just focusing on those enlisted men and women that are veterans. But creating the ecosystem and the opportunity, whether they end up in SAP, working there, I don't know. I suspect like every other person that leaves the military, 50 percent end up in another job after a year. I think that probably will be the case. But they will be ready for virtually any job I think based on their helping them with their transition.

Mr. WENSTRUP. Mr. McNerney, you are now recognized for five minutes.

Mr. MCNERNEY. I want to thank the Chairman. And I really thank the witnesses for your service and for your testimony today. It is a real bright spot in what seems sometimes can be a treacherous Committee assignment. But what I want to say is, Mr. Huseman, I want to acknowledge your 25,000 veterans goal. It is very good. How much training does it take, say, to get somebody that has no prior experience in the cloud to work on cloud activities?

Mr. HUSEMAN. In addition to our pledge to hire 25,000 veterans and military spouses, we have also pledged to train 10,000 servicemembers and veterans and military spouses in Amazon Web Services Certification. And so that is an industry-recognized certification in cloud computing. And many companies either prefer or require that you have this Amazon Web Services Certification. So companies like Netflix and GE and Adobe either prefer or require that. That commitment is valued at over $7 million. So we think in addition to hiring veterans, training them in cloud computing is also something we are very proud of.

Mr. MCNERNEY. Well, what do you think the retention is for veterans that have been through the program? In fact, you all might want to take an answer at that. Well, retention seems to be a problem with veterans in the first job or two. Do these tech opportunities look different in that regard?

Mr. HUSEMAN. Well, definitely I think building an internal support network is very important to make sure that once they are at the company that they have mentorship and career development opportunities. That is something that we have tried to focus on and make sure that we provide opportunities for employees to grown within the company.

Mr. BOWERS. I would just add that, you know, driving on the Uber platform is rather unique, because we are one of the few that are—we, of course, want people on the platform, but we aren't too focused on retention. If someone comes and drives on our platform and then ends up dropping off, it means they may have gone back to school, they may have taken advantage of an additional opportunity. So we see our numbers go up and down. A good example being our numbers right now, which are 56,000 folks who have signed up on the platform, half of those have taken a first trip. So that means there are many folks that are on the platform who haven't actually driven with Uber. But it is always there. It is ready for them should they need it at some point.

So we have kind of seen those numbers go up and down. But I will say compared to their civilian peers, veterans seem to have a much higher conversion rate than their civilian peers, which for us is a way to identify that this is a type of model that many veterans and military families really needed.

Recently the number that you mentioned, I believe other panelist mentioned was that veterans are leaving their first job out of the military after one year, it is like upwards of 50 percent I believe. The Institute of Veterans and Military Families just came out with this number not too long ago. We are often wondering if that is the franticness of veterans as they are getting out of the military to take the first job that comes their way. And it is programs such as these that my panelists are discussing that are critical to make sure that veterans are getting into these jobs where they can leverage their skill sets. So we are hoping to be able to, A, act as a buffer for folks who may be taking part in these programs, and then additionally make sure that their skill sets are being leveraged so we can get that 50 percent number down.

Mr. MCNERNEY. Good.

Mr. BERGAN. And I would love to step in here, Congressman. And I think, you know, me personally seeing firsthand and going through the MSSA program, that is one of the things that really stood out. When I sat with members of the Microsoft military community who were sharing what the program would ultimately be, they envisioned a career. And that is what really got me in that first cohort and many of my peers who went through with me. We envisioned growing with the company the same way we grew with the military. And to my testimony it has been that way for me.

Mr. MCNERNEY. So as a Committee, I mean we have a limited amount of power to help you out there. But maybe there are legislative tools that we could use that would help. If you have any of them I would like to hear them, or if you don't have them on your mind, but you would like to forward those to me, it would be very helpful to our work here. Go ahead.

Mr. HUSEMAN. You want me to take that? We have two principal recommendations. One is that servicemembers receive technical training before separation from service. When they leave the service we want them to have careers and not just jobs, technical training before separation. And even for those that aren't in technical fields, they may have an aptitude for that. And so we would encourage that.

The second thing is that we would encourage greater partnerships between the private sector and the military. We would encourage you to take a look at the Camo2Commerce Program, which is out of the Joint Base Lewis-McChord in Washington State. We have had great success with that program. For example, servicemembers who have participated in that program, they have received jobs offers from us at three times the rate that servicemembers who haven't participated in the program.

So it provides servicemembers with very valuable skills and we are—Amazon Web Services recruiters very much seek out those participants. I think that is one example of a great partnership between the private sector and the military, and I would encourage looking at the rates for that.

Mr. MCNERNEY. Thank you. Chairman?

Vice Admiral KERNAN. I think at the same time some are not going to have that opportunity to get technology training. But I think it is important that if any possibility is there, then they should. But as been already mentioned, some people don't have the time before they get out. But I do think someone alluded to the fact, hey, the Transition Assistance Program is not effective at beginning the transition of men and women in the service into the private sector. They need to talk about getting them into these Web sites and getting them going, you know, in the end of their career so they can in fact connect with commercial organizations, because most of them won't have the time and they don't know—if they get into that gap, if they leave and have no help before they leave the service, they need that help about jobs, not writing resumes, but in fact opportunities at jobs. And there are companies out there that necessarily do that. And so I think that is an important piece.

This is a government commercial—this is a commercial responsibility in my mind. It should not be necessarily a government responsibility to have to—the commercial industry is there, they are the benefactors of the veterans when they get out of the military and serve in their organizations. We just have to convince them of that and make them aware of it. And I think the program will go a long way.

Mr. WENSTRUP. Mr. Bost, you are now recognized for five minutes.

Mr. BOST. Thank you, Mr. Chairman. And I would really like to—well, first off, let me say thank you not only for those of you that served, but also thank you for providing this service. But I want to make sure, and I know we have touched on it a little bit, but there were two things that were mentioned. You can expand on those or not. But actual barriers that are blocking the opportunity for any of veterans coming out. I know one was mentioned, the Transition Assistance.

I was a radar repairman, okay. I worked up until the very last day that I separated. And trying to then all of a sudden change to think—I was lucky enough that I was going into a family business. I didn't have to be trained in that. I went home and went into the family business. But what other barriers are out there that we can actually do to help you continue to do what you are doing and make sure that our veterans are employed?

Vice Admiral KERNAN. Well, I just, you know, I think the model I think we lean on the veterans' penchant for learning and achieving and winning and succeeding and they want to do that.

So our program, there is marine infantry, army infantry, truck drivers, mechanics, all types of people. And we give them a test to see if they have a level of aptitude in software. And we fudge it a little bit to get them in there. But the fact is, when they all work together as a team, and you would be extraordinarily impressed with the diversity of the group of people, all services are represented and every class, men and women.

First they succeed together and they begin the transition together, you know, when they are moving out. And so they have a penchant to learn that. I am a knuckle dragging frogman. I had no understanding at all of technology when I got out. But I am somewhat educatable and I am leaning into this thing. And it is extraordinary to see the men and women and listen to men and women who have never done anything technology wise, albeit this generation is very savvy at technology. They picked it up, they learned it. They do it in the military all the time. And we have all experienced where you are into something that you are clueless of, but you learn it, you pick it up and you run with it.

So I don't think we cancel anybody out for moving into this opportunity. I just, you know, my stress is the, you know, first in the veterans, you know the dot org organizations, it just needs to be easy to use for a veteran. And community and companies have to partner with it so that they can have an easy time of going into it, finding where they—getting their resumes in there, finding someone to talk to. They need to talk to people, because they don't know how to transition very well. So however you can advocate for that, you know, whether it is the veteran's dot org gov site that is more usable, more user friendly.

And companies say they want to help, and so they should help. And they can easily do this I think just by investing a little bit and don't—it doesn't matter that an infantry guy, don't think an infantry guy can't roll in there and be a technology wizard. They make up for that in a lot of other qualities and they learn it very fast.

Mr. HUSEMAN. Congressman, I would also encourage the Subcommittee and DoD to look at the utilization rates for this program and how successful they are. I think the Camo2Commerce Program at Joint Base Lewis-McChord, we think, would be a valuable case study. I think figuring out how many servicemembers participate in the program, what jobs that they get after they leave service, are those jobs paying more than those in similar specialties who did not participate in those programs? We think that looking at that data and seeing what works and building upon what does work would be very important.

Mr. BOWERS. And if I could just add real quickly on the TAP component. As someone that has gone through TAP multiple times through my many deployments with the Marine Corps, I have to say it always felt like death by a thousand links. It is incredibly overwhelming for veterans to know what opportunities are out there and what tools they can leverage to be able to make that transition. And as has been mentioned by my colleagues, it is a very difficult time, very stressful time, whether it be coming back from a combat deployment as a reservist, to an Active duty member leaving the military after 20 years.

I would also ask the Committee to put some thought into something that we have realized is sort of a tangible benefit with respect to a platform such as Uber, is that veterans are able to continue to serve fellow veterans. And I speak with our partner drivers on a regular basis and hear that they want to be able to do that.

And something that we have discovered is on and around military communities, it is often difficult for partner drivers to have access on and off military installations. This is something that we are looking at as a way to reduce DUIs on and around military installations. We have met with multiple base commanders who think this would be a unique model to be able to look at. And we currently have some language as is being reviewed right now, where we would have the Department of Defense come up with these rules.

This came about because so many veterans live on and around military installations that his piqued our interest that our partner drivers came back and said, "Look, you know, I don't like the feeling I get when folks don't know that there is a tool available to keep them off the roads." You might be aware a lot of military bases you drive right outside and there is car dealerships all over the place. The reason for that is because there is a tremendous amount of—there is a lack of transportation options on these installations, which ultimately leads to servicemen and women, their families being put in a position that is a little difficult. And that is something that we believe we could alleviate.

Mr. BOST. Thank you.

Mr. WENSTRUP. Ms. Radawagen, you are now recognized for five minutes.

Ms. RADAWAGEN. Thank you, Mr. Chairman. I too would like to welcome the witnesses. Thank you for appearing today and thank you for your service. My question here is for the entire panel. Back in my home district in American Samoa 10 percent of our entire population is military veterans. My question is, what are your companies doing to ensure that our veterans who live in the United States Territories are being included in these opportunities? Could we start with Mr. Bergan?

Mr. BERGAN. Congresswoman, thank you for that question. One thing I would like to start with is being from the U.S. Virgin Islands I clearly understand that perspective. Because if I found myself going back to Virginia and then back to the United States Virgin Islands, having an opportunity like this could possibly miss me.

What I also want to highlight is Microsoft looking at the community-based model of the MSSA. And as I mentioned before we are going to follow-up with your offices to just drill down in how we get to roll that out to more places. That way our MSSA program isn't limited to the installations that it is currently on and it is serving our community at large.

Ms. RADAWAGEN. Thank you.

Mr. HUSEMAN. Yes, Congresswoman. Our hiring pledge and our training pledge to train servicemembers and veterans and military spouses in Amazon Web Services Certification is definitely open and welcome to everyone, including those in the Territories and American Samoa. We would love to come and speak with your more about that and how we can get your constituents involved in these training programs.

And I would also note that we have a number of small sellers who sell on the Amazon platform, including from American Samoa. And that is a great way, if you have a product or if you have an idea, to reach out to consumers and our customers all across the world selling via e-commerce.

Ms. RADAWAGEN. Thank you. Admiral Kernan?

Vice Admiral KERNAN. Yes. I mean our program, again, it is only two years in the making. And again, this Friday is our graduation of 22 more veterans, which puts us to 100. And we have got right around 20 states represented. We pay virtually for everything and that includes travel. The commitment is a movement for an 11-week course that we run actually here in Leesburg, Virginia. So the course is there. We actually have to fly everybody in anyway for it. They live there, they breathe there. We give them a stipend while they are there. And when they graduate they have a certification and then we can leverage the ecosystem that I discussed earlier.

So it is open virtually to anybody. It is still kind of new. So proliferating that information it is a little incredulous to a lot of people. "You mean you guys pay for everything on this thing?" Well, the answer is yes, we do. It is just—it is one model. There are lots of great models to do this. But again, I am very focused in the selection process to make sure there is diversity in terms of geography, ethnicity, the states that they come from. It is completely open to everybody anywhere and we take care of the movement of people to and from the course.

Ms. RADAWAGEN. Mr. Bowers?

Mr. BOWERS. Yes, ma'am, thank you for the question. And I would highlight if I could real quickly how young Uber is as a company. We have really only been around for about five years. And the product that our UberMILITARY program has really grown off of is Uber X, which is just about three years old. In that time, we have been able to expand to 189 cities. And we are going to continue to grown and reach out as far as we can and specifically to help veterans and military families. So I would love to be able to follow-up with you with respect to what we might be able to do in Guam specifically for vets that are there.

Ms. RADAWAGEN. Thank you, Mr. Chairman. I yield back.

Mr. WENSTRUP. Well, if there are no further questions, I want to thank you all for your testimony today as well as your thoughtful responses to our questions. I look forward to working together to not only connect our transitioning servicemembers to these opportunities at an earlier stage, but also recruiting older veterans and spouses and training them for these jobs. And I believe we all understand the positive assets that veterans bring to the table and to the civilian economy in every aspect. And I believe the tech space is a wonderful fit for many of the men and women who have served.

Admiral, I think it has probably been quite a while since your knuckles hit the ground I have to say. That would surprise me. But before we close, I do ask unanimous consent that the statements submitted for the record from the Internet Association and Engine be included in today's hearing record. Hearing no objection, so ordered. I want to thank my colleagues for being here. And finally, I ask unanimous consent that all Members have five legislative days in which to revise and extend their remarks and include any extraneous material on today's hearing. Without objection, so ordered. This hearing is now adjourned.

[Whereupon, at 2:24 p.m., the Subcommittee was adjourned.]

APPENDIX

Prepared Statement of Bernard Bergan

Thank you Chairman Wenstrup, Ranking Member Takano, and Members of the Economic Opportunity Subcommittee of the House Veteran Affairs Committee.

My name is Bernard Bergan. I am an Army veteran and a graduate of the Microsoft Software and Systems Academy (MSSA). I am also an example of how tech companies, through public/private partnerships, can make a significant impact on veterans by helping them discover meaningful career paths as they re-enter civilian life.

It is an honor to appear before the Subcommittee this afternoon to share how Microsoft has made a life-altering investment in my career and the careers of hundreds of U.S. military veterans around the country. And how after three tours of duty in Afghanistan I was able to put these skills to use at Microsoft.

Two years ago, Microsoft testified before the House Veterans' Affairs Committee to discuss how the private sector, and in particular the tech industry, could play a more hands-on role in helping our returning service members obtain the education, skills and industry-recognized certifications they need to successfully transition into civilian life with high paying careers in IT/STEM related occupations. The company had just launched the MSSA program and I was one of the first graduates. Since then I have found a home at Microsoft and the program is expanding into 12 locations around the country over the next year.

While that is certainly progress, I know from conversations with my fellow veterans that we still face enormous challenges in successfully transitioning into civilian life. Those conversations also tell me there is a real hunger among my former army colleagues for these type of skills building programs. Those of us in the private sector must provide more service members and veterans access to opportunities that will change the trajectory of their lives, like Microsoft did with me.

And I am confident that there will be many, many other graduates like me given the company's recent expansion announcement, a clear sign that Microsoft is committed to training and employing veterans for years to come. Microsoft's goal is to train and find IT jobs for 5,000 service members over the next five years.

My Story

I was born in the U.S. Virgin Islands. When I was twelve years old I moved with my parents and four brothers to Virginia where I attended high school and graduated from Old Dominion University with a criminal justice degree. I then decided to pursue an opportunity in the United States Army. I am proud to say I was on active duty from 2008 to 2014, serving all over the world, including an eleven-month deployment in Afghanistan's Helmand Province. My experience taught me the importance of teamwork, and deeply instilled the value of selfless service and a commitment to excellence.

In May 2013, after my final deployment, I returned to the United States to prepare for my transition from the Army. This was a time of uncertainty and anxiety. While there might have been opportunities, I could not see a clear path, which was frustrating.

Then I was introduced to the MSSA program by my commanding officer at JBLM, Colonel Charles Hodges. He displayed real leadership and took a chance on us; without his ongoing support, I would not be sitting before you today. The intensive IT skills training, paired with a guarantee of a job interview with Microsoft made the program my most attractive option.

The Microsoft Software and Systems Academy provided me with 16 weeks of training on the technical roles I was interested in exploring. During those four months, I realized that Microsoft was fully committed to helping me build the type of skills that would make me a valuable employee. During my time in MSSA, I met members of their Microsoft Military community who offered mentorship and support every step of the way. When I completed the MSSA program, I interviewed with Microsoft and accepted a position as a Software Developer.

Working at Microsoft has been an incredibly rewarding experience. Each day allows me to be around passionate individuals who work to have a global impact as they innovate around solving problems. The teamwork, camaraderie, and expertise I enjoy at Microsoft is similar to my time in the Army, and makes me feel more at home than I ever could have imagined when I first began the process of transitioning out of the Army.

The teamwork and camaraderie are just two of the many qualities of private sector life that are similar to what I enjoyed in the military. Others include the ability to grow. Just like in the military, I have the opportunity to earn promotions. In my case, I am especially grateful that my hard work has enabled me to be promoted twice in the two years I have been at Microsoft.

In addition to Microsoft being a good transition for me, it's also been a good one for my family. My wife has been able to refocus on her career in dental hygiene and has accepted a position with Washington State's Department of Health. She is also heading back to school to pursue her MBA. This would not have been possible had I not been able to make such a smooth transition into the civilian workforce and land my career at Microsoft.

Looking back, it is fair to say that it has not been particularly easy to transition out of the military. I was uncertain about how I would know if I was making the right career move. I wondered how I was going to provide for my family. I had no idea where we were going to live. With all of this running through my head as I tried to prepare myself for the next phase of my life, securing a high paying career in the IT industry was the farthest thing from my mind - until the MSSA program came along.

MSSA

By way of background, MSSA is a joint effort of Microsoft and its educational partner, Embry Riddle Aeronautical University (ERAU). The two have been hard at work collaborating with military installations such as Joint Base Lewis-McChord (JBLM), Camp Pendleton, Fort Hood, and Fort Campbell to implement the Microsoft Software and Systems Academy across the country. The company has also developed an ecosystem of private sector employers that have stepped up to hire MSSA graduates.

I am pleased to report the program has graduated more than 325 veterans from JBLM, Fort Hood and Camp Pendleton, of which 92% are presently working in high paying STEM related careers in the IT industry with an average starting salary of more than $70,000. Microsoft has plans to bring the program to an additional eight communities over the next eighteen months, servicing 14 military installations across the country. Fort Benning will open next in early August, followed by Marine Corps Base Quantico, Fort Bragg, Fort Bliss, and Marine Corps Base Lejeune in the months to come. Over one hundred employers, including some in this room, have joined with Microsoft to hire MSSA graduates into high paying tech careers. Their partnership is critical to the long-term success of this effort. I am proud to be a part of that success, because I have seen how the MSSA program changes lives for the better.

I have come to find out through my work at Microsoft and by talking with my fellow MSSA graduates, employers outside of the IT sector are also competing for this same talent. Great companies from a wide spectrum of industries like GE, Ford, JP Morgan, Deloitte, and Blue Cross have stepped up to hire significant numbers of veterans.

Given the enormity of the challenge, Microsoft understood they could not do this alone and that this initiative was not just about feeding their company talent pipeline. In fact, the skills that I have acquired were not Microsoft specific, but rather industry recognized credentials that provided me with job portability to work in a wide variety of rewarding IT occupations. More work is required to provide greater access to these skills training and job opportunities.

As I mentioned earlier in my testimony, over the next five years Microsoft is committed to graduating 1,000 transitioning veterans each year, and placing at least 90% of them into high- paying jobs in the IT industry. We recognize that some MSSA graduates will decide to pursue their degree with the credits earned in the program. I know this option is also a viable path to employment success and should be supported through polices in Washington, D.C.

Though our veteran unemployment rate has seen a significant drop, we are not yet out of the woods. With more than 200,000 veterans planning to transition out of the military every year over the next five years, there is a big opportunity for the IT industry to tap into a large talent pool of agile, dedicated, and technically sharp workers. These veterans continue to face unique challenges in transitioning to the civilian workforce, and deserve the highest level of support.

I think my experience in transitioning was quite similar to many others; simply put, the transition to civilian life can be overwhelming and brutally challenging. There are numerous obstacles to overcome - an entirely new culture, a new language, and a new environment. Any one of these can be hard to manage on their own; together, they are very difficult to overcome. While there are hundreds of veteran support programs already in existence, the key differentiator of the MSSA program is that it prepared me for the whole host of transition challenges that face a veteran. While the four hours of technical homework every evening gave me skills that let me interview for the Microsoft job, what makes this program stand out from all others is the soft-skills training. I learned to write a resume; conduct myself in an interview; dress appropriately in a business setting; and develop an elevator pitch. But the most important part of this process was connecting with a veteran mentor from Microsoft. He checked in with me on a weekly basis, and we chatted about what life would be like once I transitioned out of the military. He shared his personal stories about how he overcame challenges with the help of the military affairs community that exists at Microsoft.

SkillBridge

As I am sure the Members of this Subcommittee know very well, the Department of Defense, through its SkillBridge program, permits transitioning veterans to begin a certification or vocational training program such as the Microsoft Software and Systems Academy. From my experience, it was a life changing opportunity.

This skills training can take place during a service member's last six months in service, affording the service member relevant training in a field he/she wants to pursue, and possibly securing employment prior to their end-of-active service (EAS). While this DOD program is beginning to gain momentum, there continues to be a preference for utilizing that transitioning service member until the very last day of service due to operational tempo and command requirements. This places an undue burden on the service member and restricts their opportunity to pursue career paths that can lead to high-paying jobs in industries I never believed possible. I urge the Members of this Subcommittee to work with the DOD and their military base commanders to broaden the acceptance of SkillBridge programs across a greater number of bases across the country. As a practical matter, there could also be a substantial cost savings for the military as more and more service members are able to secure meaningful civilian employment thereby reducing unemployment insurance costs for their respective branch of service. In these tight fiscal times, DOD could potentially save tens of millions of dollars annually by incorporating these successful programs onto every base in the country moving forward, and I'd recommend this committee to encourage the Department in that direction.

National Cybersecurity Employment Forecast

I'd also recommend this committee engage with technology companies encouraging them to train and hire veterans in new areas, like cybersecurity, where demand is high. It is no surprise to most in this room that the Bureau of Labor Statistics continues to project a significant shortage of critical IT workers over the next decade. One very important technical area, where skilled workers are in most demand, is cybersecurity. These workers are critical, not only to the IT industry, but also to the public sector where they help protect our nation's infrastructure (electrical grids, waterways, mass transit, etc.). Transitioning service members with cybersecurity skills and top security clearances are primed for these high-paying careers. For our part, over the next several months, Microsoft will add a Security Administration Learning Path to the MSSA program, so that those who are interested in a career in cybersecurity can gain the training they need.

Community-Based Model

While much of my testimony has focused on veteran employment, it is also important to understand military spouses. Spouses make tremendous sacrifices, especially when their loved one is deployed, protecting our nation and its citizens all over the world.

For its part, Microsoft recognizes that more must be done to help spouses, and to that end, the company will be establishing a community-based model of our Microsoft Software and Systems Academy (MSSA), that will offer evening courses, making them more available to working spouses who may want to make a career change.

These two community based MSSA models will launch within the next 12 months in San Diego and Jacksonville. While we are also eager to expand into Norfolk, another vibrant military community with a significant number of active, retired and veteran military population, the Navy's higher operational tempo and need to keep their sailors working through their last day of service is making the launch of a model there more difficult than anticipated. But with the Committee's support and encouragement, we are hopeful that individuals in the Navy will soon be afforded similar opportunities, and possibly have a great IT career awaiting them at the end of their military service.

Conclusion

I am so proud of the work the Microsoft Military Affairs team is doing to empower veterans like me with training that leads to high-paying IT careers.

Our veterans are a national resource. As a nation, we invest in them heavily with the best training and most technically advanced equipment in the world. These are smart, agile, dependable, and motivated individuals that are ready to work. It is incumbent upon all of us to facilitate the challenging transition from the military to the civilian workforce.

Our veterans have made sacrifices. It is time for industry, government, and nonprofit leaders to give back by investing in our veterans by increasing access to the types of in-demand IT training that leads not just to a job, but to meaningful careers. The Microsoft Software and Systems Academy is a model that fulfills this mission. I am living proof.

Thank you for your ongoing support of our veterans and for allowing me to share my story and Microsoft's commitment.

APPENDIX FOR BERNARD BERGAN'S TESTIMONY

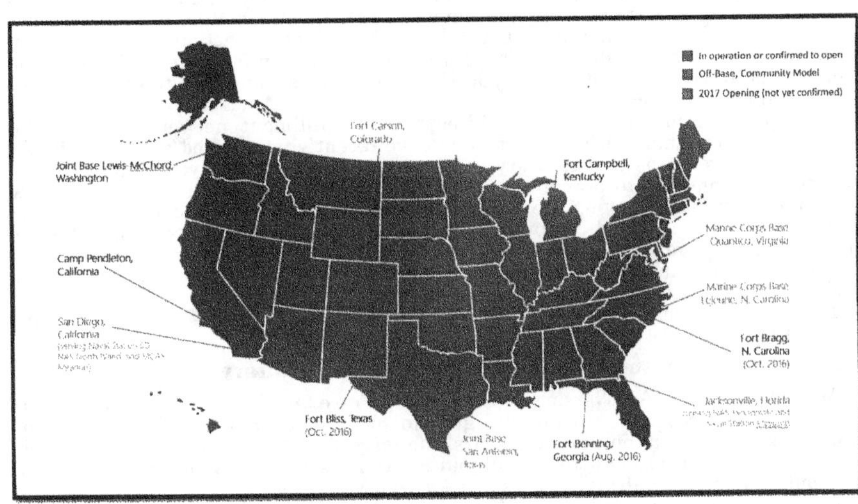

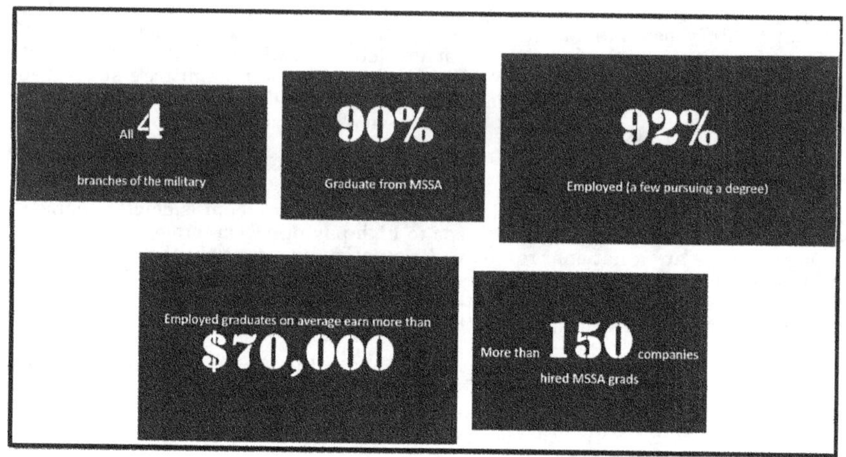

Prepared Statement of Brian Huseman

Thank you, Chairman Wenstrup and Ranking Member Takano. My name is Brian Huseman, and I am Amazon's Vice President of Public Policy. Amazon's mission is to be Earth's most customer-centric company. To accomplish this, we're constantly looking for leaders who can invent, think big, have bias for action, and deliver results on behalf of our customers. These principles look very familiar to the men and women who have served our country in the armed forces - and also to their spouses.

Amazon actively recruits U.S. military veterans to join Amazon to fill roles across our company, from our corporate offices to our fulfillment network. Since 2011, we've hired more than 10,000 veterans, and we recently announced a major commitment to hire veterans and military spouses over the next five years. In addition, Amazon is committed to providing technical training to service members, veterans, and military spouses, paving the way for them to secure the certifications necessary to pursue careers in cloud computing, where open positions outpace hiring. We believe this is the smart thing to do for our veterans and military spouses, for Amazon, and for our hundreds of millions of customers - and we're excited to keep hiring and training these incredible leaders.

Thank you for your attention to this important topic, for calling this hearing, and for inviting me to testify.

I. Amazon's Commitment to Hiring Veterans and Military Spouses

As part of the 5th Anniversary of the Joining Forces initiative earlier this month, Amazon announced that we are pledging to hire 25,000 additional veterans and military spouses over the next five years, the largest pledge announced by any technology company. These new hires will join Amazon's growing community of veterans and military spouses, also known as our Amazon Warriors.

At Amazon, we're guided by our *Leadership Principles*. [1] They're ingrained in our work - we use them when we're talking through a new project, interviewing a prospective hire, or solving a customer's problem. What we've found in our years of hiring veterans and military spouses is that many of our Leadership Principles closely align with what makes people successful in the military.

While our pledge is stepping up our commitment to hiring veterans and military spouses, Amazon has a well-established history of actively recruiting and developing candidates from the military. Amazon's Military Talent Partnership is a team of military recruiters that includes veterans from all branches of the armed forces. Our team assists applicants in translating their skills and experience to the requirements of job openings at Amazon and provides them guidance for how to successfully interview. Amazon recruiters attended more than 70 veterans job fairs in the last year to help veterans and military spouses find job opportunities at Amazon. Our team works hard to provide veterans and military spouses with opportunities and the tools to pursue successful careers at Amazon.

---

[1] See https://www.amazon.jobs/principles.

We are also fortunate to have a strong and growing group of military spouses on our team. We've found that military spouses' calm under regular change - paired with their ability to handle ambiguity - make them well-suited for the fast-paced, ever-changing work at Amazon. Military spouses face the significant challenge of finding careers that can move with them through frequent relocations with their spouses. For example, our Virtual Contact Centers offer a unique customer service work experience that enables our associates to work remotely. This provides consistent, meaningful work for military spouses, and allows Amazon to employ highly capable customer service representatives across the country.

This is the promise of the growing tech industry, after all - creating the flexibility of position portability, and empowering military spouses to pursue careers, not just jobs. We're proud of our military spouses, such as Gen Harrison-Doss, whose husband is stationed at Dyess Air Force Base. Gen leads a team of recruiters in Seattle from her home in Abilene, Texas, and has not only moved during her tenure, she has been promoted and continues to advance her career at Amazon.

II. Training and Mentorship of our Veteran Employees

Our commitment to the military does not end once candidates are hired. Once employed at Amazon, we offer veterans several programs that help them transition more easily into the civilian workforce. We connect them with our significant internal network of veterans to provide mentoring and support. Our Amazon Warriors employee affinity group provides a community for veterans and military families to share experiences, gain exposure to career and development opportunities, and participate in community and recruiting events.

A. Amazon Web Services Certification Training

As part of our recent Joining Forces announcement, we also pledged to train 10,000 service members, veterans, and military spouses in cloud computing - offering a path to Amazon Web Services (AWS) Certification and providing a gateway into this high-demand field. AWS Certifications recognize IT professionals with the technical skills and expertise to design, deploy, and operate applications and infrastructure on AWS.

Successfully passing AWS Certification requires hands-on experience with the AWS Platform. So through our pledge, we are offering these 10,000 transitioning military service members and spouses free membership to AWS Educate, a critical resource to accelerate cloud-related learning endeavors. AWS Educate provides training courses, a wide library of cloud content, and access to our collaboration portal. We will also offer free access to labs that are part of the examination preparation programs. Finally, AWS Certification exam fees are eligible for reimbursement from the Department of Veterans Administration under the GI Bill's education provision.

B. Career Choice Program

Veterans and military spouses in eligible Amazon roles can enroll in the Amazon Career Choice Program, where we'll pre-pay 95% of tuition and fees for courses related to in-demand fields, regardless of whether the skills are relevant to a career at Amazon. Through this program, we exclusively fund education in high-demand fields, as defined by the U.S. Bureau of Labor Statistics.

Last year, we expanded the initiative to include purpose-built classrooms onsite at eight of our U.S. fulfillment centers. We found that offering courses onsite helped associates be more successful in achieving their aspirations at Amazon or beyond. With this in mind, our new fulfillment centers will be built with onsite classrooms as part of the standard blueprint, and we're bringing dedicated onsite Career Choice Classrooms to more than a dozen existing sites.

So far, thousands of employees worldwide have participated in Amazon's Career Choice program, and our first Career Choice graduate is now a registered nurse in Kentucky. We are proud of this innovative program and the fact that our current and future eligible veteran and military spouse employees will have the opportunity to earn certificates and associate degrees in such fields as aircraft mechanics, computer-aided design, machine tool technologies, medical lab technologies, and many others.

III. Recommendations for Increasing Veterans in Tech

Because of our extensive experience in hiring veterans and military spouses, we would like to offer two principal recommendations for increasing the number of veterans in the tech sector and better preparing them for a transition to the industry.

First, we recommend that the military offer active duty service members the ability to partake in technical training in fields like cloud computing before they depart from service. Although the U.S. has the most technically advanced military in the world, our service members may not be working with the latest software and systems that are being used by the private sector. We also believe many separating service members are excellent candidates for careers in high-tech, even though their backgrounds might not be technical. Without any technical training, they may never explore jobs in this high-demand field. When veterans transition, many don't have the flexibility to invest in education and training that will lead to a better career. Often, the first job they're offered is the one they will accept. We believe technical training programs during their military service will mean our veterans can enter the job market fully qualified to be hired at tech companies like Amazon.

Initiatives such as the Department of Defense (DoD) SkillBridge Program provide an opportunity for service members to pursue critical training prior to separation from service. Under this program, some service members can participate in civilian job and employment training - including apprenticeships and internships at tech companies - up to six months prior to service separation. Use of this program is not widespread due to the operational demands of the military. Amazon recommends that the Subcommittee explore the program's utilization rates and identify whether this program could be expanded without negative effects on staffing availability and unit readiness.

Second, we also recommend expansion of partnerships between the military and the private sector that can prepare our service members for jobs in the technology sector. Specifically, we recommend expanding the Department of Defense (DoD) Training/Education with Industry (TWI/EWI) and Secretary of Defense Corporate Fellows Programs (SDCFP). Since 2013, Amazon has partnered with DoD in sponsoring select military personnel to spend a year in the TWI/EWI program. And for the first time, we'll also be participating in SDCFP. Amazon offers our TWI/EWI students and SDCFP Fellows an exceptional, world-class experience by providing exposure across our many business segments and activities. This year, eight commissioned officers and one senior non-commissioned officer (two Air Force, four Army, and three Navy) were assigned across Amazon business units - including our fulfillment centers, operations, Prime Air, and Amazon Web Services. These service members - as well as those placed at other companies - are exposed to new processes and innovative business cultures during their time at tech companies. They're able to bring back new ideas and try different processes when they return to service. And in return, companies like Amazon have top-tier military talent offering new perspectives on our business and how to connect with customers. We recommend that other technology companies make the investment to partner with the DoD on this successful program, which has proven its value to both Amazon and the DoD.

We also recommend more programs like the Camo2Commerce program. Camo2Commerce is a career development initiative that assists transitioning service members from Joint Base Lewis-McChord in Amazon's home state of Washington. The goal of this program is to enable transitioning service members to move into the civilian workforce, and specifically into high-demand, well-paying career opportunities, such as cloud computing, through one-on-one career coaching, job placement services, short-term training, and hiring fairs. We have found that the service members from Camo2Commerce are more likely to have the skills required for Amazon's technical positions. And our AWS hiring managers seek out service members who have completed Camo2Commerce. We hope programs like Camo2Commerce will be expanded and replicated to other bases.

Conclusion

Amazon looks forward to working with you and our tech industry colleagues to increase the number of veterans in the tech space and to ensure they have the right skills when they are ready to transition out of the military. Our veteran and military spouse employees are a tremendous asset for our company and our customers, and we are excited to see what the next 25,000 who join Amazon will build and innovate over the next several years.

Thank you again for inviting me to testify. I look forward to your questions.

Prepared Statement of Vice Admiral Joseph Kernan (U.S. Navy, Ret.)

Chairman Wenstrup, Ranking Member Takano and Members of the Subcommittee. My name is Joseph Kernan. I am a retired U.S. Navy Vice Admiral - having spent over 36 years on active duty. I am currently the Senior Vice President of Corporate Development and Marketing for SAP National Security Services. But

I am here today to testify in my other role as Chairman of NS2 Serves, a non-profit training and employment program for veterans.

It is an honor to appear before you today to talk about an issue that is very important to me - the successful transitioning of our military service members into the civilian workplace. As you will see today, I am very passionate about this topic and this subcommittee has my heartfelt thanks for its continued work in assisting veterans returning home.

My commitment to this issue stems from my years serving in the US Navy. After graduating from the US Naval Academy in 1977, I spent my years on active duty developing deep experience in naval, joint and special operations and in government interagency and national security matters. After serving at sea on Navy warships for 4 years, I transitioned to the SEAL program in 1981 and served in each of six geographic regions and in all Naval Special Warfare leadership career milestone positions. These include commanding SEAL Team Two, the Naval Special Warfare Development Group and the Naval Special Warfare Command - overseeing all resourcing, readiness and employment requirements for the SEAL/Naval Special Warfare community. I recommissioned and served as Commander of the United States Fourth Fleet, overseeing US and foreign counterpart naval activities in the Caribbean and Central and South America - my final career tours were as the Senior Military Assistant to former Defense Secretary Robert Gates and Deputy Commander, US Southern Command.

Today's veteran

Veterans have chosen to devote a portion of their lives to public service. During their service, they develop a wide variety of work and life skills that are invaluable in the civilian workplace. The challenge of translating these skills when applying for a job or at the workplace is often daunting for the aforementioned veteran population. These young men and women do not want a handout, but rather an opportunity for a fresh start in post-military life and a chance for a fulfilling career. Unquestionably, this can help mitigate many of the personal challenges veterans face as a result of the traumas they may have experienced in conflict zones.

The commercial information technology field is ideally suited to veterans, regardless of their military occupational specialty. For example, service men and women routinely use commercial technology to manage mission planning, human resource management, systems operations and maintenance, and supply chain and financial management functions common in the commercial business sector, This, combined with the generational trend to leverage technology for everyday activities, ideally suits veterans for work in the I.T. field. It is important for employers to understand that veterans not only serve our country's national security interests but as well must run the day-to-day business of the Department of Defense.

The personal traits and attributes developed over the course of service in the military are truly the extraordinary commercial work place differentiators. From the very start of their military service, young men and women are instilled with a strong sense of character and develop invaluable work traits:

1. Veterans strive to be leaders.

In the military, leadership is continually fostered to the point of becoming an ingrained attribute. Veterans respect and understand the roles of leaders and willingly accept and seek leadership opportunities. Very importantly, there is a clear understanding of the preeminent responsibility of those entrusted with leadership roles. They learn from some of this nation's best leaders - allowing these veterans to become successful leaders themselves.

2. Veterans know how to work as a team.

Working successfully in a team is an essential attribute in an effective workplace. It is also the foundation on which safe and successful military operations are conducted. Veterans have developed an uncompromising responsibility to their peers, subordinates and superiors alike. Veterans have learned to work indifferently and respectfully with teammates and co-workers, regardless of race, gender, religion, ethnicity and national origin. They understand that there is "no 'I' in team" and that success is invariably related to their collective efforts. While military duties stress teamwork and group productivity, they also build individuals who are able to perform independently when the situation demands it.

3. Veterans are trained to quickly learn new skills and concepts.

While in the service, members of the military are continually trained in a multitude of cross-functional skills and routinely become adept at mastering the tools that enable success. The demand for both administrative and occupational skills is high, and the ability to quickly adapt to dynamic operational environments or emerging technology enhancements is essential to mission success. The risk and dire consequences of complacency are well understood by every veteran.

4. Veterans are mission/goal oriented.

In the military, the mission is paramount. Veterans have been trained to plan extensively for a particular task and adapt to the circumstances they face during mission execution. Their sense of duty, responsibility and accountability for job performance and mission success are not compromised and remain priorities. The culture, leadership and proficiency within our military are respected and envied around the world.

5. Veterans excel in high stress situations.

In today's fast paced work environment, having the ability to persevere under difficult or stressful circumstances is critical. Veterans are trained and expected to perform under stress, accomplishing assigned tasks in a timely and effective manner. They learn to do so with the resources at hand.

6. Veterans are highly effectively in a structured environment.

Companies may hesitate to hire a veteran, believing their military experiences don't translate to a corporate setting. To the contrary, veterans have a deep sense of accountability and they understand how policies and procedures are necessary for stability, safety, and productivity. They are able to follow rules and schedules, and value organization and discipline.

7. Veterans have strong communication skills.

Finally, regardless of varying intellectual and physical abilities, each individual is respected for his or her role in the organization. Military personnel are taught to have a questioning and thoughtful mentality, and they are not afraid to respectfully offer perspective and recommendations to supervisors.

NS2 Serves

In order to help address the challenge of unemployment among young veterans, SAP National Security Services Inc. r (SAP NS2r) - an independent subsidiary of SAP SE, comprised of U.S. citizens operating on U.S. soil - established a non-profit organization in 2014, NS2 Serves, to train and find employment for veterans in high-tech careers. SAP NS2 is the predominant funder for this program - but we continue to look for partners within the business and philanthropic community.

Through this program, predominantly targeting enlisted men and women from all military services and skill specialties, we arm graduates with SAP technology certifications and other attributes highly sought by commercial human resource managers and others in the technology arena. The NS2 Serves program is unique in nature and there are a number of key distinguishers worth mentioning. I have attached a document to my statement with specific details and qualifications for the NS2 Serves program - but let me highlight them for you today.

- First, the program specifically targets enlisted men and women rather than the officer corps, who tend to have far fewer problems finding post-service employment. Unemployment continues to plague many veterans once they leave the military, particularly in the case of enlisted men and women between the ages of 25 and 34. The Bureau of Labor Statistics reported in 2014 that the unemployment rate for veterans was 25 percent higher than the nonveteran unemployment rate - and that statistic has stayed fairly consistent over time. Unlike veteran hiring programs marketed by many companies, which as well have many benefits, NS2 Serves targets younger veterans who have recently left military service or are in the process of leaving the military and are most challenged finding substantive employment. Despite their years of dedicated service, younger veterans are struggling to secure full time, substantive career opportunities to support themselves and their families.
- Second, the program is an in-resident, fully funded, 11-week program that leverages veterans' penchant for teamwork. By having an in-resident program, participants can collectively help each other in the transition and through the challenging academic regimen without other day-to-day demands and distractions associated with commuter or part-time programs. Invariably, participants develop a strong friendships and personal commitment to the success of every member of the class. Many hours are spent outside the classroom studying to ensure this goal is met. Ultimately, the class measures their individual success by the success of the entire class.

- Third, each graduate receives a highly valued industry consultant certification and skill set which, to date, has afforded 100% job placement and a minimum starting salary of $60K, inclusive of family medical and retirement benefits. Select companies that have hired our veterans include: SAP NS2, SAP, Accenture Federal, US Department of Agriculture, Deloitte, Lockheed Martin, Northrop Grumman, CBeyondata, Johnson Technology Systems, Inc., Defense Logistics Agency, Naval Supply Systems Command, and Unisys. The certification that the graduates receive to support SAP software offers them vast employment opportunities within the government and in the private sector. Thousands of companies and organizations worldwide utilize SAP products and require support from trained consultants.
- Fourth, and finally, the program training positions graduates not only for a career in the IT field but also equips them with the relevant skills necessary to branch into many other lines of work. A veteran's military service and military experience - coupled with the NS2 Program training - affords employers with a devoted employee that can become a highly productive member of an organization.

The average NS2 Serves class size ranges from 19 - 23 veterans. By the end of this week, we will have graduated 100 veterans and to date, have successfully helped 100 percent of our graduates gain employment. Our cost per graduate of the program is approximately $15,000 and we feel this is a worthwhile investment in our nation's veterans.

The NS2 Serves program metric is not about gross numbers of veterans hired into any jobs or numbers hired that have deep military, industry or educational backgrounds. The program targets those with the greatest need, provides them with a high demand, career-centric skill set, and then places graduates in jobs that start careers. The program's success requires all of these components.

Recommendations for the increased hiring of veterans

Since beginning the NS2 Serves Program in 2014, I, and all those at SAP NS2 that voluntarily support the program, have learned much about the continued challenges facing today's veterans.

One of the most important lessons we have learned is that training and placing veterans in jobs that have strong career potential mitigates many of the personal and emotional challenges veterans often face. The horrors of war have taken a great toll on this generation. They need substantive, rewarding work to care for themselves and their families that might negate a future dependence on government subsidies.

As I've stated, programs targeting the hiring of veterans must address the needs of those most challenged to find post-military service employment. In order to help posture veterans for success in transition, the provision of some level of education and training can be critical. This is certainly the case for those jobs that offer strong career potential but the investment does not have to be exorbitant, as veterans are masters at on the job training.

Virtual Job Opportunity Forum

At present, most veterans do not have an understanding of the civilian hiring process nor do they have access to the information that would facilitate their search efforts. A central, easily accessible repository/website of job opportunities and application guidelines would be useful and the Department of Labor's "veterans.gov" website can be a start. However, even this particular online tool can be difficult to navigate. The user has to know the right keywords to input in order to get useful information. In addition, if the user does not use the correct keywords, their resume can be rejected - similar to what frequently happens with the USA Jobs site.

Far too often, veterans looking for employment are overwhelmed by the process and our goal should be to make these kinds of websites easy to use. Prior to the end of their service, veterans should be exposed to this type of tool. This central repository should be populated by the numerous companies that market their intent to hire veterans and must be continually updated in order to be useful and relevant to veterans entering the job market.

Investing in veterans

With so many veterans looking for employment and with limited resources to assist them - we have to find ways to more effectively connect veterans to job opportunities. I would ask that there be strong advocacy for the NS2 Serves model - invest in preparing veterans and give them the entry skills they might need for a particular job. Many companies have the resources to support this model and should be proactive in this regard. They just need to recognize the long term value of veterans in their workforce.

Job qualifications

Most enlisted veterans leaving the service do not have college degrees, often a requirement for securing a career-promising job. Veterans should be recognized for their significant experience. Those programs which give veterans college credits for what they have learned and experienced are extremely helpful. Each veteran who has attended the NS2 Serves program is pursuing their college degree. Their GI Bill benefits are critical to this goal. A key component to the value of the NS2 Serves program is that government or GI Bill benefits are not required for completion. Rather, the program model is for potential employers to invest nominally in veterans so they are can begin their post-service careers.

Conclusion

Mr. Chairman, Ranking Member Takano and Members of this Subcommittee, I would again like to thank you for the opportunity to testify before you today. As you can tell, I feel very strongly that more needs to be done to prepare today's veterans for entering into the civilian workplace. Today's veterans have so much more to offer this country. Our task is to help harness their talents and assist them along the way.

I am happy to answer any questions you may have for me today.

Prepared Statement of Todd Bowers

Chairman Wenstrup, Ranking Member Takano, and Members of the Committee. Thank you for inviting me to speak to you about the UberMILITARY program and our endeavors to support veterans and military families as they face the many transitions that military life offers. It has been many years since I last sat before this committee and I am honored to be invited back.

I would like to take a few moments to first share with you how I ended up becoming involved in the UberMILITARY program. I served as a Marine Reservist for more than 12 years here in our nation's capital. During my enlistment, I deployed multiple times finding myself crossing the bridges of Al Nasiriyah and in the streets of Fallujah, Iraq. I've climbed the mountains of northern Helmand province in Afghanistan and shook hands in small villages in South America. Not a day goes by that I am not thankful for these experiences and how it shaped me into who I am today.

It was during my second tour in Iraq that I was caught in a firefight that pinned me behind a HMMWV (Humvee) on the outskirts of Fallujah just prior to Operation Phantom Fury. Unexpectedly, the vehicle that I was taking cover behind drove off the roadway leaving me exposed to enemy fire. With my cover suddenly gone, I engaged a machine gun position and was struck in the face by a sniper's bullet as it skimmed through my rifle scope. Needless to say, the Marine that drove the HMMWV away did not get a 5 star rating for that trip.

A few months later, I found myself back in Washington D.C. waiting for classes to start. To make ends meet, and avoid depleting my hard earned deployment savings, I worked difficult hours at a local bar and took on a work study program. The inability to have a flexible work schedule negatively impacted my studies greatly. It was during this time, that I realized there had to be a better way for my fellow veterans to find some financial stability with opportunities that provide the flexibility and mobility that vets need to face the many rigors of reintegration into civilian life. This is what inevitably led me to UberMILITARY.

In September 2014, Uber announced that we were aiming to partner with 50,000 members of the military community including veterans and military family members. We created this target because we knew that the skills, work ethic, and integrity exemplified by our nation's veterans is unmatched - frankly, we knew it would be good for business. Based on data tracking in cities with high veteran populations, like San Diego, our data showed that compared to their civilian peers, veteran partner drivers drove on the Uber platform longer and had higher customer ratings. Focusing on veterans and military families was a business decision but more importantly, it was a way to empower this community.

After just 18 months of engaging with the military community, Uber achieved its goal and ahead of schedule. Today, more than 55,000 self-identified veterans and military family members have signed up to drive with Uber and over 50% have taken a trip on the platform. All of that work has resulted in an astounding $152,000,000 in earnings.

To mark this moment, Uber has donated $1,000,000 on behalf of our uberMILITARY Advisory Board to organizations that support veterans and military families, including the USO, The Fisher House, Tragedy Assistance Program for Survivors (TAPS) and Iraq and Afghanistan Veterans of America (IAVA).

So how did Uber do this? To start, we designated and engaged with more than 60 UberMILITARY program leaders from our city-based teams, many of which are veterans themselves. These individuals led the charge in their respective cities working with local and national organizations, base commanders and community leaders. We launched country-wide rider and driver UberMILITARY awareness campaigns, and hosted a Veterans Day in-app activation in support of the White House Joining Forces Initiative to help homeless veterans get to and from employment opportunities. We tightened up our military identification and verification process for those already on the platform to ensure we could continue to effectively engage with them. Then to take our program even further, we partnered with blue chip organizations that support the military community such as the Chamber of Commerce Hiring Our Heroes initiative, Blue Star Families and the American Military Families Association.

Finally, Uber created the UberMILITARY Board of Advisors, an impressive group of military leaders chaired by former Secretary of Defense Dr. Robert Gates, to provide guidance on this important project. General Stanley McChrystal, Admiral Michael Mullen, General James Mattis and Mrs. Sheila Casey are just a few of the others that signed on to lend their support and currently serve on our Board of Advisors.

We couldn't be more grateful for those who have advised and partnered with us to help make our goal become a reality.

After engaging with active UberMILITARY partners, we found that veterans and military families are particularly drawn to driving on the Uber platform because of the flexibility it offers. In fact, in a March 2016 UberMILITARY driver's survey, 77% of those surveyed stated that they decide when to drive with Uber, and schedule it around their other commitments. For most veterans, that flexibility provides an opportunity to readjust to working and interacting with civilians. But for some veterans, specifically those who have disabilities that require more care, it allows them to earn income while still being able to easily make time for medical appointments and other therapies that are essential to their recovery. We believe we offer veterans a new type of transitional experience that will set them up for the success they deserve.

Being an Uber partner gives our nation's veterans economic freedom, a chance to be their own boss and even allows them to leverage one of their largest assets, their cars. Our survey of UberMILITARY partners informed us that the number one reason veterans sign up to drive is to earn money as a secondary source of income. This feedback came as no surprise given the results of the most recent Veteran Affairs Economic Study, which found that 53% of separating Post-9/11 veterans will face a period of unemployment. Driving with Uber helps to conveniently and easily fill these gaps for veterans as well as their families.

Many veterans find themselves in a rush to find work as they begin to transition back to civilian life. As I experienced in my own transition, when there is not an immediate income opportunity available it is very easy to get into a spiral that leads to burning through savings, incurring debt and mounting bills creating a financial urgency that forces too many to take the first job offer that comes their way. The Institute of Veterans and Military Families recently concluded that "nearly half of those surveyed stayed in their first post-separation position 12 months or less. Further, there is an association between job tenure and job alignment with the respondent's preferred career field." If veterans feel pressure to find employment immediately they tend to accept employment that may not effectively leverage their skill set resulting in low retention rates. Uber provides an alternative path for veterans - one where they can take their time finding a job without the burden of financial stressors.

UberMILITARY allows our transitioning veterans the flexibility they need to successfully adjust to civilian life, provides economic opportunity, fills the gaps of unemployment that too many experience, and gives them the time to figure out what they really want to do without the burden of financial stressors. But UberMILITARY is not just providing opportunities for veterans, we are also actively recruiting military family members. Blue Star Families' most recent Military Lifestyle survey highlighted that 58% of non-employed military spouses would like to be employed or have some source of income. Finding consistent employment that allows flexibility and is transferable to other locations around the world has never been so readily available, and now military spouses and family members are being empowered by driving on the platform. We are so proud to be able to provide opportunities for military families that, at times, felt left behind by an employment marketplace that didn't fit their lifestyles.

Admiral Michael Mullen, former Chairman of the Joints Chiefs of Staff, once said that driving with Uber "...provides flexibility and allows veterans to pursue the American dream, be it furthering education, pursuing certification or starting a small business. It's a tremendous platform for those transitioning from the military." And that is exactly what I hope UberMILITARY can do, help our veterans pursue their American dream.

As we look at the future for UberMILITARY, we are setting new goals that will continue to have an impact that this community has earned and deserves. Our new mission is as follows:

- **$500M in earnings to driver partners who have served in the military and their families by 2020:** We want our UberMILITARY veterans and families to take home half a billion dollars by 2020 throughout their work as driver partners.
- **Increase access to reliable transportation in military communities and reduce alcohol-related incidents on and around military installations.** UberMILITARY is going to focus on making transportation more accessible around military installations by reaching out and working with base commanders and community leaders to ensure that everyone has a safe ride. By expanding access to reliable rides at the push of a button, we hope to see a reduction in alcohol-related incidents in military communities. We look forward to expanding our partnership with Mothers Against Drunk Driving (MADD) to provide safety education programs on and around military installations.
- **Make Uber even more rewarding for drivers from military backgrounds.** We are currently expanding existing programs to offer unique rewards specifically for members of the UberMILITARY family.

I would like to conclude my testimony today on a personal note. After leaving service, I knew I wanted to do something that would truly make a difference in the lives of my fellow service members and I can tell you that I am fulfilling my dream by being a part of UberMILITARY. The flexibility and earning opportunity that driving with Uber provides allows veterans and military families to support their many transitions, generate additional income and support their families and communities in ways never before possible. I am proud to say that a technology platform has never economically empowered this community in such a manner before, and this is just the beginning. As we continue our mission, I am enthusiastic to go to work every day and help provide the opportunities that our veterans and military families deserve.

Thank you for your time and I look forward to answering any question you may have.

Statements For The Record

INTERNET ASSOCIATION

May 13, 2016

The Honorable Brad Wenstrup
Chairman
Subcommittee on Economic Opportunity
House Committee on Veterans Affairs
335 Cannon House Office Building
Washington, D.C. 20515

The Honorable Mark Takano
Ranking Member
Subcommittee on Economic Opportunity
House Committee on Veterans Affairs
335 Cannon House Office Building
Washington, D.C. 20515

RE: "Veterans in Tech: Innovative Careers for All Generations of Veterans."

Dear Chairman Wenstrup and Ranking Member Takano:

The Internet Association applauds your efforts to highlight the work that Internet companies do for transitioning veterans. We appreciate the opportunity to provide a written statement for the hearing on "Veterans in Tech: Innovative Careers for All Generations of Veterans" and request that this letter and attachment be submitted for the hearing record.

The Internet Association works to advance policies that foster innovation, promote economic growth, and empower people through the free and open Internet. The Internet creates unprecedented benefits for society, and as the voice of the world's leading Internet companies, we ensure stakeholders understand these benefits.

Our men and women in uniform return home with invaluable skills: they are some of the most highly qualified and trained individuals in the nation, equipped with unique skillsets and leadership that enhance diverse backgrounds. In addition to recognizing the value of veterans' skills in the workforce, Internet companies also recognize that the connected world offers new opportunities for transitioning veterans to harness new skills. To build upon both of these opportunities, Internet companies are undertaking new and creative methods of providing our veterans with the tools they need for a successful future.

Diverse Internet platforms offer an array of opportunities and tools for veterans in transition. While the experience of each platform and veteran is unique, several observations regarding the opportunities provided by Internet companies include:

1. The sharing economy has created flexible workforce opportunities for today's veterans, allowing them to create their own schedules and be their own boss.

2. As veterans return to the workforce, a standard nine to five regime may not fit their needs. These new Internet platforms help to ease the transition back into the workforce by offering flexible options.

3. Internet companies provide veterans with unprecedented access to global resources that provide support for veterans and their families.

4. Veterans are equipped with unique and valuable skills that enhance the workforce within Internet companies.

As hundreds of thousands of men and women transition from military life each year, Internet companies look forward to working with our partners and veterans to continue and build upon the success of current programs. Attached to this letter, please find description of just some of programs offered and supported by Internet Association companies. We commend your attention to this issue and look forward to continuing to work with you to advance opportunities and support networks for our nation's veterans.

Respectfully Submitted,

Michael Beckerman
President & CEO

CC: The Honorable Jeff Miller, Chairman, House Committee on Veterans Affairs
The Honorable Corrine Brown, Ranking Member, House Committee on Veterans Affairs

Attachment

Airbnb

The Airbnb Open Homes program provides free, short-term stays on Airbnb for individuals and families during times of need or celebration such as medical patients traveling for treatment, low-income students visiting college campuses or veterans transitioning to civilian life. Airbnb works with nonprofit organizations to identify the guests. Thanks to Airbnb's incredible host community, they are able to not just provide these individuals with a place to stay; they are able to offer them a place to call home during a time of need, celebration or adventure. Through this program, Airbnb has worked with organizations like The Honor Foundation and Operation Code to provide free accommodations for military veterans traveling for job interviews and professional development opportunities.

In addition to internal programs, Airbnb has donated to veteran aid efforts in the community. On November 22, 2014, Airbnb donated $77,000 to Swords to Plowshares to complete the funding for new housing for veterans at The Stanford Hotel on 250 Kearny Street in San Francisco. Airbnb also provided funds and volunteer hours to put finishing touches on the space with furniture, paint and decoration.

Bevan Dufty, San Francisco's Director of HOPE (Housing Opportunity, Partnerships and Engagement) said, "Airbnb is providing needed people-power and financial support to ready 250 Kearny for 130 veterans who no longer have to live on the streets of San Francisco. [...] Our goal is to end veteran homelessness and Airbnb is helping us make a giant step towards that goal."

Michael Blecker, Executive Director of Swords to Plowshares said, "Transforming 250 Kearny Street into housing for homeless veterans has been a true community-wide effort. [...] Airbnb's generosity and commitment to giving back to our community is an impressive example of how the private sector is stepping up to help Swords to Plowshares and the city end veteran homelessness."

CPO and co-founder of Airbnb, Joe Gebbia, made it clear that, "Airbnb is honored to support our hometown heroes who have selflessly served our nation [...] We are pleased to commit resources and bring our community of employees, hosts and guests together to help ensure that 250 Kearny is a welcoming home for San Francisco's Veterans."

Facebook

Social media has dramatically changed how servicemen and servicewomen stay in touch with their families and friends. Over the last four years, military families have significantly increased their use of social media. In fact, 93% of military families currently use Facebook to stay connected which is why Facebook is committed to making the lives of veterans easier.

Facebook is a long time sponsor of the Blue Star Families Military Lifestyle Survey. As such, Facebook works with BSF to facilitate a holistic understanding of service members, veterans, and military family experiences so that communities, legislators, and policymakers can better serve the military population's unique needs; and identify the key aspects of military life to effectively target resources, services, and programs that support the sustainability of military service and the All-Volunteer Force.

In addition to finding high numbers of military families using Facebook to stay connected, this year's survey found that the percentage of military family members (for example military spouses) who have considered suicide (10%) is almost equal to the percentage of service members who have considered suicide (9 %). Facebook already provides suicide prevention resources and tools. Specifically, friends can report suicidal content, which triggers an email to the poster, providing him/her with a note that includes contact and chat information for the National Suicide Prevention Lifeline.

Veterans, active duty service members and their families can have special needs. BSF has been working to meet these needs and there are several specific resources provided to our nation's military that BSF wanted to make sure they were aware of, especially in times of potential crisis. That's why BSF worked with the Facebook engineering team to develop a customized solution that could help to identify military families and military personnel, ensuring that friends and family members could send critical military-related counseling information to them in times of need.

Today, BSF, Facebook, and the Department of Veterans Affairs are proud to announce that the Facebook military crisis content is live. As a result, friends and families with concerns about veterans, active duty service members and military family members will receive specific information about crisis services for our nation's military including The Veterans Crisis Line. The Veterans Crisis line connects veterans in crisis and their families and friends with qualified, caring Department of Veterans Affairs responders via phone, online chat or text messaging.

This is just one way to help our nation's military families in their time of need. However, we believe that the Facebook platform, which is used on a daily basis by so many of our families, will be a critical means of helping our military community live long, healthy and successful lives after they have sacrificed so much for our safety and way of life.

On February 25th, 2016, in partnership with Blue Star Families and USAA, Facebook released the Military Families Online Safety Guide designed specifically for their service members and their families. The Military Families Online Safety Guide delves into how to utilize Facebook's privacy, security, and safety tools to do things such as enable additional security features, block someone from seeing what veterans post, or report something inappropriate. The guide also addresses situations unique to military families, for example, sharing seemingly innocuous personal information and how that could inadvertently conflict with good security procedures.

Facebook also proudly supports Blue Star Families (BSF) by consistently providing annual sponsorship of BSF's Annual Neighbor Celebration in Washington, DC. This April was the 6th anniversary of the celebration which honors civilians with awards for helping and supporting veterans. The goal of the event is to bridge the gap between veteran and civilian communities.

Lastly, in 2015, Facebook launched a series of Boost Your Business events geared towards helping Veteran and Military family-owned and operated small businesses learn how to reach new customers and keep existing ones through Facebook. Since then, Facebook has reached more than 1,000 Veteran and Military family-owned and operated small businesses in four states, partnering with more than 65 local and national Veteran and Military family-focused business organizations. Facebook plans to continue hosting these events through 2016 and beyond.

Google

In the summer of 2013, Google hosted resume writing workshops for 350+ student veterans in 12 Google offices in partnership with Student Veterans of America and Iraq and Afghanistan Veterans of America. In November 2013, working collaboratively with the Bob Woodruff Foundation, Google welcomed more than 100 injured post-9/11 veterans and their loved ones to Google NYC for a tech immersion and mentoring day. Finally, VetNet, the Google+ career services platform with the Institute for Veterans and Military Families and Hire Heroes USA, has helped thousands of veterans prepare for civilian careers.

VetNet, or the Google Veterans Network was launched in 2012. VetNet is an internal employee resource group and volunteer community that strives to make Google a great place to work for employees who have served, as well as their families, friends and supporters. Google also supports the active duty and military veteran community outside of Google through a wide range of transition-related programs and partnerships. Their mission is to conduct operations around the world to attract, recruit, and retain top veteran talent to Google, provide a Google support and learning network, and help solve challenges in the veterans community with Google products.

Different aspects of The Google Veterans Network are making available apps like Helpouts by Google and Tour Builder and sharing stories from veteran-owned businesses via the Google Enterprise blog and Google+.

Helpouts by Google allows anyone to give and receive help over live video, and Google thinks it can be an effective platform for nonprofit and veteran service organizations to connect with veterans and their families. Helpouts for veterans are already available, ranging from guidance for veteran education benefits to entrepreneurship/business planning. Because Helpouts is HIPAA-compliant, providers such as Give an Hour can provide secure and confidential mental health care sessions online-particularly useful for those veterans who are physically unable to travel from their homes.

Tour Builder is a storytelling tool in beta that enables anyone to record memories of their travels in Google Earth. Tour Builder was inspired by the accomplishments of military service members around the globe. Google hopes it will give veterans an easy way to share their journeys with loved ones at home and to preserve the legacy of their service for generations to come.

13.5 percent of the nation's businesses are run by veterans, employing a collective 8.2 million people. In recognition of the contributions veterans make to the economy, the Google Enterprise blog and Google+ page will share stories throughout the week from veteran-owned business and service organizations that achieved success with the help of Google Apps-like RuckPack Combat Nutrition.

LinkedIn

LinkedIn allows veterans to reach their full potential by connecting them with opportunities at a massive scale. LinkedIn offers veterans free subscriptions to Lynda.com, an online learning platform with over 4,000 businesses, technical and creative courses taught by industry experts available anytime and anywhere. To harness the unique skillets of veterans, Lynda.com's course offerings include programs on personal branding, entrepreneurship, management, and technical skills. Lynda.com helps veterans build the skills essential to transition into a post-military career, connecting two million veterans with nine million companies and five million job opportunities, in addition to hosting numerous military and veteran focused groups including the Veteran Mentor Network which has over 100,000 members.

Lyft

On Veterans Day 2015, Lyft teamed up with the White House initiative Joining Forces to offer thousands of free rides to homeless veterans, administered by local VSO employment counselors. In order to accomplish their goal, Lyft worked in tandem with Uber to maximize the number of free rides that would be available to veterans.

According to Colonel Nicole Malachowski, the executive director of the Joining Forces Initiative, "veteran employment has always been a focus for Joining Forces," however, it is difficult for homeless veterans to find transportation to and from work due to limited public transportation. Colonel Malachowski spoke for Joining Forces and First Lady Michelle Obama when she directly thanked Lyft on Veteran's Day 2015, "for stepping up to help address this problem," and for being "committed to donating free rides to veterans - to be administered by the employment counselors who work with them every week."

Monster

Monster Worldwide Inc. has been a global online employment solution for more than 20 years. Over the years Monster expanded from their roots as a "job board" to a global provider of a full array of job seeking, career management, recruitment and talent management products and services.

In 2004 Monster Worldwide and Military.com joined forces with a shared commitment to provide resources and information to connect service members, veterans, and their families to all the benefits earned in service and to help them make the most of their military careers, transition to the civilian workforce and improve their lives.

In addition to providing resources to help service members and veterans navigate the policies and procedures for claiming their benefits, Monster and Military.com developed a collection of veteran transition tools and products for both the private sector and the federal government.

In 2007 Military.com worked with the Department of Defense to create TurboTAP, the first online transition program. TurboTAP enabled active duty service members and members of the National Guard and Reserve to create Individual Transition Plans (ITP). Members were able to create, download, and print customized guides to help them plan and track their transition progress; equipping them to achieve their civilian career goals. Military.com continues to support this important time through the Transition Assistance Center.

Following the advent of the Post-9/11 GI Bill in 2008, Military.com developed the first online GI Bill calculator designed to help veterans determine which of the several GI Bill programs would best fit their personal needs.

In 2011 Military.com and Monster's Government Solutions division, developed the military skills translator and job matching tool for the Department of Veterans Affairs 'VA4Vets' website.

The patent pending tool goes beyond simply helping service members and veterans translate their military occupation into civilian terms and match them to current employment opportunities; it also helps them to see new employment and career possibilities beyond their current expectations.

The military skills translator/job matcher is currently being used by more than 50 corporations, veteran service organizations, and trade associations to help connect veterans and employers. Of course all of the tools and products on Military.com are free for veterans, service members, and their families.

This year Monster increased their efforts to help veteran job seekers by overhauling the entire job seeking process on Military.com and developing new tools and products to help veterans "find better."

As a result of the renewed efforts, Military.com will soon launch the Military.com/Citibank transition app, the first of many new veteran employment focused apps to be released in the future. Military.com recently launch an updated and enhanced Military Skills Translator/Job Matcher. Future enhancements will include the addition of an academic factor, which will enable veterans to find jobs that match both their military and academic skills and experience.

Monster will continue to demonstrate their commitment to making a positive impact on the lives of those who serve or have served, by continuing to develop new ways to connect employers and veterans.

The Veteran Employment Center is a all-encompassing job resource that helps employers to hire Veterans with Military.com integrated product offerings. Employers can diversify their recruitment strategy and connect with millions of Veterans, Transitioning Service members and Military Spouses on one single Veteran Hiring platform.

Transition by Military.com keeps active duty service members and reserve and guard personnel on point during their journey from military to civilian life. The app provides a 360-degree view of transition including financial, benefits and job-related content, pushing timely information 18 months prior to separation and for 6 months after. The app personalizes your transition plan tracking your progress while you complete the interactive checklist items which include required Department of Defense out-processing paperwork.

The Veteran Employer Resource Center offers comprehensive information to reach job seekers with Military experience and helps you to be on the forefront of veteran recruiting. It is a one stop shop for all employers to learn about the benefits of hiring veterans and about how to recruit and retain them. This will be launched in June 2016.

Pandora

Pandora is working with a few organizations on future collaborations to get more military veterans in their applicant pool. This includes reaching out to ROTC chapters for Pandora's summer RoadCrew internship program for college juniors. Tim Westergren, the Founder and CEO of Pandora, feels strongly about building outreach efforts to military veterans, which is part of their overarching diversity strategy.

In March 2016, Tim Westergren gave a speech to 1,200 freshman cadets and faculty as part of the West Point Military Academy's Castle Lecture series. His speech focused on commitment, technology, entrepreneurialism, and innovation.

On May 6th, 2016, Pandora participated in a recruitment event at the Service Academy Career Center (SACC) in Washington, DC, the only job fair exclusively for service academy alumni.

Currently, Pandora is collaborating with Musicians on Call, an organization founded in 1999 that brings music to hospital patients, on future visits to Veterans Affairs facilities.

Salesforce

Over the next 5 years, over one million service men and women are expected to transition out of the military (at a rate of approximately 200k each year), and many will experience difficulties in readjusting to civilian life. One major hurdle that veterans face is finding meaningful careers. Many have a great foundational skills from the military, but need additional training to find the best available opportunities in the civilian workforce.

Salesforce believes that the thousands of U.S. veterans transitioning from the military each month are some of the hardest working and dedicated individuals. They come with solid teamwork, communication, critical-thinking, and problem solving skills.

Due to the large volume of veterans entering the workforce and Saleforce's commitment to helping them adjust to civilian life, Salesforce launched their new and improved global program, VetForce Community in March 2016.

VetForce Community is a holistic learning experience that addresses critical gaps in the veteran's journey. Its mission is to transform the lives of veterans and military spouses by free training, certification and connections to employment opportunities in the Salesforce ecosystem, which currently has thousands of customers and partners. VetForce prepares veterans for a civilian career in IT, consulting, or sales. Salesforce recognizes the skills, experience, and aptitude that veterans gained as service members, and combine those with business skills and Salesforce training to get veterans ready for the civilian workforce.

Salesforce has incorporated ideas and input from many veterans across all military branches to build out this program. As a result, Salesforce offers complete and supported learning journeys that teach veterans the skills needed for a career as a Salesforce Administrator, Business Analyst, Developer, or Sales Rep.

The redesigned platform now includes career-specific learning journeys, immersion in Trailhead, business skills training, partnerships with the Developer and MVP communities, a veteran coaching program, robust job prep resources and employer engagement with Salesforce's customers and partners.

The process is self-paced and on-demand making VetForce easy for veterans to use. Users begin by learning about Salesforce careers and selecting a career to start their learning journey. Salesforce goes beyond the basic job description and provides detailed career overviews for Salesforce positions. Salesforce also notes relevant skills and experience from the military that are relevant for each job role. After choosing a career, the learning journeys include six phases.

The first phase is the orientation phase where veterans learn about day-in-the-life for their chosen career and get connected to support resources for their journey, like online collaboration groups and regional user groups.

In phase 2, Veterans dive into Salesforce training on Trailhead, where they complete a series of self-paced training modules that teach them the fundamentals and gives them hands-on experience setting up and configuring their own Salesforce application.

Phase 3 gives Veterans the opportunity to brush up on their Business Skills. VetForce covers the essentials like business email communication, running effective meetings, great presentations, whiteboarding, and time management.

In phase 4, veterans can take their training to the next level by attending optional in-person training cohorts.

Phase 5 is all about getting Salesforce certified. Veterans are guided through the certification process, reviewing study guides, certification prep blog articles, and receiving their free voucher for the certification exam. Getting certified boosts their career and enables veterans to contribute even more to an organization's success. Salesforce Certification is the ultimate credential from Salesforce that demonstrates that they have the skills and confidence to take full advantage of Salesforce.

Lastly, in phase 6, veterans update their LinkedIn Profiles, create their resumes, and review the Job Search Kit that includes sample interview questions, interview prep tips, and questions to ask during the interview.

Currently, Salesforce has over 2,500 members in the VetForce Community that include currently serving, veterans, military spouses, VSOs, employer partners, and coaches. VetForce Community members have earned over 1,000 badges on Trailhead and over 150 certifications. With Trailhead integrated in the VetForce Community, veterans are now able to take thousands of hours of free Salesforce training to jumpstart their tech industry careers.

Due to this success, VetForce's FY17 goal is to train, certify and employ 5,000 veterans and military spouses and Salesforce hopes to achieve 40,000 in 2020.

In order for this goal to be reached, Salesforce aims to include the entire Salesforce ecosystem, and is working with their Customers and Partners to provide employment opportunities for veterans and spouses who complete their training and certification. Salesforce also actively engages one of their greatest assets - the Admin, Developer, and Salesforce MVP communities, to ensure veterans are supported throughout their learning journey.

Zenefits

Part and parcel to the Zenefits platform is helping small business owners start, manage, and grow their business; and provide quality benefits normally reserved for employees at large employers. One of those benefits is the brokerage of insurance (health and life). As Zenefits grew the company, they added traditional experienced brokers to their team and trained new brokers to enter the industry. An industry that has seen far fewer new entrants to it's community over the last several years.

In order to train these new brokers, Zenefits developed Zenefits' Brokers University. As they began to think through their Veteran's pledge Zenefits made the decision to begin providing training for Veterans to become brokers.

Zenefits is currently working with the White House, the Governor's office in Arizona and others to make spots available in our Broker's University this summer to Veterans in the Phoenix area. Zenefits will train these individuals to become successful brokers in Arizona and pass their licensing exam. Some will work for Zenefits, some will go work for Zenefits' competitors, but all will have the opportunity to train in a field that is now more needed than ever.

Engine

May 17, 2016
The Honorable Brad Wenstrup
Chairman
Committee on Veterans' Affairs
Subcommittee on Economic Opportunity
U.S. House of Representatives
Washington, DC 20515

The Honorable Mark Takano
Ranking Member
Committee on Veterans' Affairs
Subcommittee on Economic Opportunity
U.S. House of Representatives
Washington, DC 20515

Dear Chairman Wenstrup and Ranking Member Takano:

Engine commends you for holding today's hearing entitled "Veterans in Tech: Innovative Careers for All Generations of Veterans." Engine is a non-profit organization that supports high-growth, high-tech startups through research, advocacy, and policy analysis. We work to foster and promote forward-looking government policies that support today's high-tech economy.

One of the most consistent challenges for startups at every stage is finding employees with the necessary skills to build innovative products and services. We know this from conversations with startup leaders around the country and we have seen this in the numbers: the Department of Labor expects STEM fields to yield more than 1.3 million job openings by 2022. Even today, there are over half a million un-filled jobs in information technology across all sectors of the economy.

Meanwhile, over 2.6 million post 9/11 veterans are transitioning back to civilian life, returning to communities around the country in search of new careers. Because of their flexibility and low barriers to entry, emerging on-demand services, such as Uber, have already proven to provide good, part-time jobs for veterans in search of more permanent work. We hope these opportunities represent pathways to the tech industry, where veterans can either build on the skills they already have or acquire new skills they can deploy. Trained as leaders and decision makers in complex situations, many veterans have the fundamentals to quickly learn or adapt problem-solving skills as an entrepreneur launching a startup or an engineer at a fast-paced tech company.

Unfortunately, many veterans interested in entering the tech industry as full-time employees-or even as entrepreneurs-are not receiving sufficient training and exposure to opportunities in this sector. We have heard directly from veterans that the Transition Assistance Program gravely lacks up-to-date information about the vast job opportunities in the tech sector and that the program does not adequately provide veterans with the resources and training necessary to pursue those jobs.

The Engine team has had the fortune of working with a number of exemplary non-profit organizations around the country that are stepping in to help veterans access these opportunities. One such veteran-founded organization, VetTechTrek, exposes veterans to tech jobs at growing startups and is building a video platform to prepare them for landing jobs at these companies. Another group, Vets in Tech, runs eight national chapters that coordinate training programs with major technology firms including SalesForce and Microsoft. The COMMIT Foundation funds technical training programs not covered by veterans' GI benefits, which raises another issue Congress should address. Each of these organizations plays an important role in connecting and training veterans for roles in technology.

Even once veterans identify the relevant training they need to pursue jobs in the tech industry, their GI benefits may not help them cover the costs. Federal funding guidelines make it particularly difficult for veterans to access non-traditional, skill-based education programs that are relatively new to the education landscape, but are already producing success stories. Training programs like coding bootcamps teach students the technical skills needed for transitioning to work in fast-growing tech fields, and at a faster pace and lower cost than traditional two- and four-year colleges and universities. Not only can these programs provide skills that bridge military experience with roles in the private sector, but they also provide the tech vocabulary and network that enable veterans to land desirable jobs.

As Congress considers how it can best support veterans in this new, tech-driven economy, Engine hopes lawmakers explore two issues, in particular. First, lawmakers should investigate how the Department of Veterans Affairs can modernize the Transition Assistance Program to better prepare veterans for this country's most in-demand jobs. Further, Congress should explore how to integrate emerging third-party educational opportunities, such as coding bootcamps, into existing educational offerings covered by GI benefits. The VA's Accelerated Learning Program pilot is an important first step towards evaluating such programs and determining the extent to which the government should facilitate veterans' participation.

We already know that our nation's veterans possess the skills and the drive necessary to become successful in the tech industry. Last year, we profiled seven former servicemen and women who transitioned to the tech industry as employees at major tech companies and as founders of their own tech startups. Together, these men and women showcase the enormous potential within the veteran community to serve and lead in our country's most rapidly growing job sector. Yet to accelerate these successes and enable more veterans to enter into this industry, we must do more.

Sincerely,

Evan Engstrom
Executive Director, Engine

○